The ~~Hardest~~ *Smartest*-Working Person in the Room

The (often-hilarious) guide to efficiency for principals and other leaders

Spencer Allen, EdD

1st Edition 2025

Publisher: Redux Publishing
ISBN: (Paperback)

DEDICATION

To my principal friends in the Diocese of Jefferson City

Contents

Contents 5

Introduction: The Smartest-Working Person in the Room 7

Closing the Open Door: Setting Boundaries with Office Time 23

To-Do or Not To-Do? Time Blocking 41

Battling the Hydra: Embracing an Inbox-Zero Mindset 57

All Together Now! Organizational Communication Best Practices 71

2001: An Office Space Odyssey: A.I. as an Efficiency Tool 87

Leadership Isn't a One-Man Band: Transformative Delegation 111

Longer than You Think! Efficient and Effective Meetings 129

From Compliance to Coaching: Effective Instructional Leadership 147

Conclusion: Finding Balance 173

The Eight Themes of Leadership Efficiency 177

About the Author 179

References 181

INTRODUCTION

THE SMARTEST-WORKING PERSON IN THE ROOM

It is not enough to be busy; so are the ants. The question is: What are we busy about?

-Henry David Thoreau

Let's get to the point. If you're reading this book, you probably *don't have time* to read a book. You're in good company! It doesn't feel like I should have time to write it, either. People in my social and professional circles often tell me that I seem to be the busiest person they know.

I'm not.

Earlier in my career, that might have been true, but now my aspiration is to be the most *productive* person I can be while maintaining balance in my life.

Part of this journey involved distancing myself from empty distractions, such as by reducing my interaction with social media and television. But the game changer has been an increased intentionality in how I approach my projects and responsibilities.

As argued in other books on productivity, such as Tim Ferriss's *The 4-Hour Workweek*—productivity is not synonymous with busyness.[i]

If you've picked up this book, chances are that your candle is burning at both ends and you're finding it hard to carve out a moment to catch your breath.

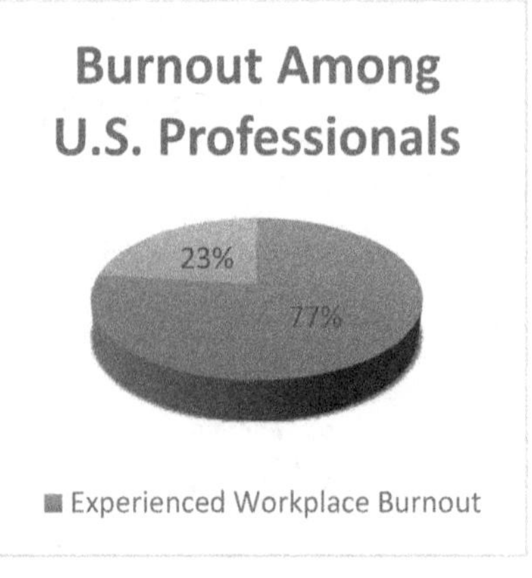

You might be concerned you are compromising your health, as well as important relationships and your sense of professional fulfillment.

Your stress needle is either pegged at burnout or creeping steadily toward the red.

The American workforce, including those in leadership positions, are notoriously overworked. In a survey of 1,000 U.S. professionals, consulting group Deloitte found that 77% of respondents reported experiencing workplace burnout.[ii]

The word *efficiency* carries a nasty connotation. An abridged version of *The Grapes of Wrath* is more efficient, but what would the book be without a whole chapter about a turtle crossing the road? Fast food fits into a busy schedule, but an expanded waistline doesn't fit into our pants. Texting "Luv U" is efficient, but it doesn't come packaged in snuggles and smooches.

Efficiency shouldn't be about compromising quality, but zeroing in on the most important things, sweeping everything else out of the way.

This book is primarily aimed at school principals and other

Throughout this book, *PROTIP* boxes such as this will give additional suggestions that reflect best practices related to the chapter's content.

Roman numeral superscript (i, ii, iii ...) in the text indicates endnotes that contain the full citation for any research or references.

The footnotes, indicated by Arabic subscript (1, 2, 3 ...) are generally more casual commentary that doesn't fit the flow of the main text.

The *often-hilarious* parts of the book, as promised in the subtitle, can be found in the footnotes. And even this was a concession. The upright editors at Redux Publishing only allowed the bottom-margin comments at all under the condition that I included the following legalese: *Readers are advised not to read the footnotes, which are juvenile and sometimes subversive.*

school system administrators. However, my hope is that readers from other industries will find the advice useful, as well.[1]

So, if you aren't in education, keep reading. Let's learn from each other. Even the chapter eight discussion of

---

[1] Just quick note of appreciation that you decided to join me down here in the gutter to read the footnotes. I promise, only two or three of them are subversive. As I argued in my conversation with the folks at Redux, most books on efficiency are hilarious. Case in point, the seminal work by Gordon H. Sputtle, CPA, MBA: *Efficiency: 176 Pages on Efficiency*. Here's one zinger from Sputtle's work: "I optimized my workflow so well, I tried deducting time spent blinking. The IRS didn't see it that way."

instructional leadership is really a discussion of how transformative leadership increases the efficiency and effectiveness of an organization.

No matter what one's professional role, time—like money—answers to the laws of economics. Many of us are trying to spend more energy and hours than we have. The exhaustion you feel is a type of bankruptcy. It may seem that the last thing you need right now is a book to read.

No worries! I'll keep these chapters as focused as possible. After all, we both have work to do, and our inbox is filling up like a spaceship full of Tribbles.[2]

The ~~Hardest~~ Smartest Person in the Room[3]

"They aren't making any more of it," Mark Twain wrote about land. That's not necessarily true–just look at Dubai. But our time is limited. The economy of minutes and hours doesn't care about your mental health, your professional growth, or your daughter's dance recital.

But *you* should care about those things.

One of my former colleagues had an email signature that read, "My goal is to be the hardest-working one in the room." While I respect this individual, I couldn't connect with the signature line, so I modified it to title this book. Our goal is to be the *smartest-working* person in the room.

---

[2] Let's pause here a moment while the younger readers look up "Tribbles."

[3] My subtitle is also a nod to another powerful book on efficiency: *The 25-Minute Heart Transplant* by Dr. Vance "Snippy" Delmar, M.D. His subtitle: *The Fastest Blade in the Room.*

I am in no place to judge whether this professional had a healthy life balance, but being the *hardest-working* person in the room seems like a dangerous aspiration. After all, think of the popular expressions for a "hardest-working" mentality. Working like a dog.[4] Sweating blood. Breaking one's back. Some days we find ourselves running on fumes because we've burned all of the midnight oil.

Efficiency isn't going to solve any problems if it doesn't involve shifting your perspective of time and responsibility. While it takes a lot of intentionality at first, implementing the best practices in the following chapters will eventually become more intuitive. "Successful people are simply those with successful habits," writes Brian Tracy, the author of *No Excuses: The Power of Self-Discipline*.[iii]

Being overworked and overstressed can be a symptom of a workplace with systemic problems. But it is often a sign of poor self-discipline or a miscalibration of one's attitude toward task completion.

In addition to introducing the principles that guide *effective* efficiency, this book will conclude with a discussion of balance. Just being efficient doesn't solve any problems if the space you free up isn't then filled with positive experiences and habits.

You have to be the one to care about those things and make decisions based on your value system.

Like many individuals in human services careers, educators often embrace martyrdom for the sake of their students.

---

[4] Maybe we should strike *working like a dog* from the list. My dog is currently taking one of 18 naps she has scheduled for the day.

The exhaustion school leaders feel is amplified by the weight of perfunctory tasks and low-impact responsibilities.

A longitudinal study by Grissom, et al. (2013) found that, because of my administrative tasks, many principals spend less than two percent of their time working with teachers on instruction and curriculum.

The hardest-working person in the room embraces these tasks. The smartest-working person in the room finds ways to minimize the impact of tasks on time and energy.

Value-Based Prioritization

Earlier this school year, shortly after writing this chapter and the next, I began to experience some burn-out and a general listlessness. After an inventory of my professional value system, I realized that I was allowing clutter and busyness back into my professional routine.

Excellence in our careers should never come at the expense of our well-being and our presence in the lives of those we care about.

Through much of my administrative journey, I've valued face time with my team, but this year was an especially busy one. We were going through a major expansion project and an accreditation process. Several positions needed to be filled for next year, and on top of this, I'd decided to visit the frontlines of instruction by teaching a creative writing class for a year.

Without realizing it, I had given myself over to what author and researcher Kim Marshall calls *hyperactive superficial principal syndrome* (HSPS), which happens when principals prioritize tasks over instructional leadership.

Principals model the values and priorities of the school program through the decisions that we make. By taking a step back to take stock of my role and how I had been serving the school, I was able to recalibrate in my daily schedule.

The organizer below is intended to help you think through how your responsibilities align with your value system. Use this tool to take inventory of some of your professional responsibilities, organized by the value you place on them.

The decreased width of each section in the organizer

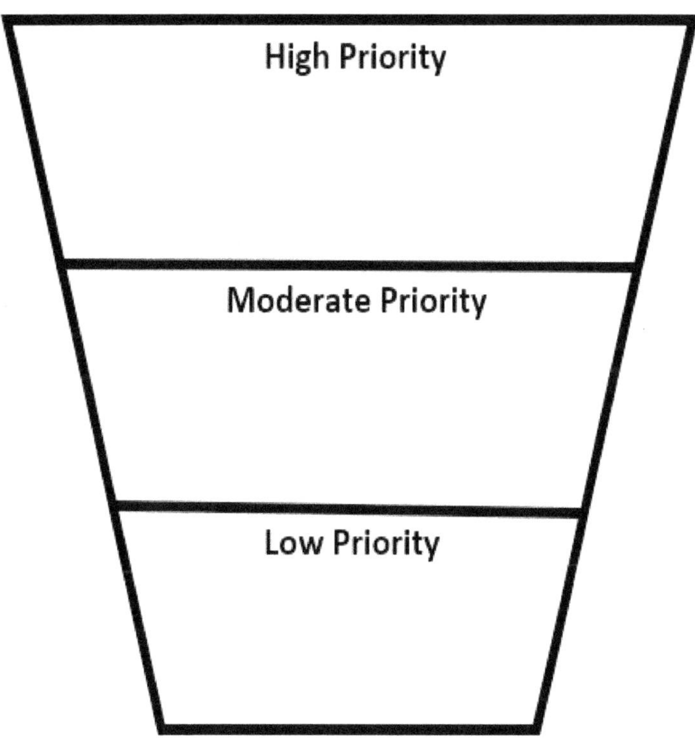

represents the amount of time that you should spend on these responsibilities.

Often, *when* and *to what extent* one commits to certain tasks might not always be under that individual's control, but set those challenges aside for this activity. For now, we are simply envisioning an ideal prioritization.

In the top section of my own diagram, I included teacher observations and instructional coaching. Not only do these activities are central to my role as a principal, but I believe that instructional leadership should happen intentionally *every day*.

Along with observations, principals should prioritize opportunities to visit with teacher teams and check in during professional learning community discussions, keeping a finger on the pulse of collaborative discussions about student work and common assessments.

Visibility among students and staff also went into this top section for me. Meetings straddled the line between high and moderate priority. Chapter six will explore how meetings are key to reinforcing the school's mission.

In the middle section, I included items like writing thank you cards, responding to important emails, and handling student discipline. Although not a daily task, I also consider it at least a medium priority to stay on top of professional learning and connecting with colleagues about what workshops, reading, or podcasts they've tapped into lately.

While these items are all important to me and essential to my role, they might not happen every day, or I consider them to play a supporting role in pursuit of instructional excellence and healthy culture.

In the bottom section, I listed paperwork, most of my email queue, and lunch or dismissal duties. These are often nonnegotiable parts of the job, but their impact on our daily schedules should be minimized as much as possible.

Efficiency and Transformational Leadership

The exercise above was intended to help readers take stock of their roles. What we do with our time defines our purpose.

You are not a task master.

Rather, you are an instructional leader. An architect of culture.

Even those readers who are not from an educator's background recognize that transformational leadership does not take place from behind a desk.

Efficiency isn't about comprising quality, but zeroing in on the most important things.

When I recently gave a talk on efficiency, some of the principals in attendance remained behind to discuss my talk and the challenges in their schools.

However, one of them rationalized, a lot of the issues he dealt with were possibly caused or exacerbated *because* his daily responsibilities kept him from being among his community. Problems festered and new ones emerged.

He was right. Being present in the classrooms and hallways

won't necessarily solve all of the culture issues you might be facing. But my experience is that the presence of strong and positive leadership among young people and teachers drastically improves culture and instruction.

When the principal has the energy and time to inspire, coach, and model, the entire school benefits.

This is especially true when principals have a healthy perception of their abilities to effect change. In my research and experience networking with other school leaders, improvements in culture, instructional quality, and student achievement appear to correlate, not just with a principal's visibility, but with a strong sense of self-efficacy.[iv]

However, administrative tasks, such as emails and paperwork, often crowd out one's ability to focus on more impactful goals, potentially reducing the extent to which principals feel they can influence the quality of their programs.

A quick internet search on time efficiency will turn up a number of suggestions, including to-do lists, automation of tasks, and delegation. Often, though, such suggestions are presented superficially or based on faulty assumptions.

The chapters that ahead are filled with practical, rubber-meets-the-road suggestions. But the guidance is based on eight key principles for shifting how you view your role as a leader in excellence and architect of culture.

Each recommendation is based upon an underlying principle that has led to a shift in perspective that I have made in my life and that I suggest you make in yours. Those principles will be highlighted at the start of each chapter.

Some of the ideas in this book are a bit counter-intuitive, starting with chapter one. I'll either hook you or lose you with that chapter, but if you stick with me, we'll take a journey that goes beyond simple efficiency hacks.

Systemic Obstacles and Archaic Visions

Each spring, a local bank invites our top students to visit with the bank president and others from the management team over lunch in the executive dining room.

Last school year, somewhere between salad and dessert, one of our hosts explained to the students how much banking culture has changed over the last few decades.

Many school systems and other organizations have structures and policies that decrease efficiency and effectiveness for instructional leaders.

"When I started here," he said, "getting ahead meant being the first one here in the mornings and the last one to leave."

Our host at the bank luncheon continued on, though, to explain that his organization, like many others, had evolved to recognize that employees and those who lead them need balance in their lives.

Unfortunately, many of us operate within similar systems, working long hours out of a sense of duty, our days bogged down with desk work and meetings.

Often, school leaders must adhere to policies or expectations that create obstacles to efficiency. One former principal shared with me that, during the latter part of her career, she had been reprimanded twice for not being at her desk when her supervisor visited the building.

Where had she been instead? In classrooms, observing teachers. But her supervisor's opinion was that she should always be at her desk, managing the building.

The role of school principals is going through a shift, even if many school systems have not caught up. The role of principal is so much more than student discipline and putter-outer of fires. We have come a long way from the model of Mr. Belding and Principal Skinner.

However, evolution is a slow process. Some readers face systemic challenges to efficiency and effectiveness, such as school systems that have guidelines that dictate how teacher observations and coaching should look. This might inhibit one's ability to explore the coaching-based observation model explored in chapter eight.

Many schools also have limited resources, including tight budgets. As a result, principals in this situation often juggle many roles, leaving very little time for instructional leadership.

Unfortunately, nothing in this book can solve all of these organizational challenges. The best solution I can offer is to pass the book along to the individuals who *can* solve embedded obstacles to efficiency within a system.

A conversation about value-based school leadership should involve policy-makers within an organization, such as superintendents and boards, just as much as it should include teachers and other staff. At the very least, these individuals may gain some insight into efficiency, as well.

I started thinking a lot about writing this book during the professional slump I mentioned earlier in this introduction. I was going through the motions and neglecting meaningful contact with my school community.

Often, I write as a way to realign my compass. I believe strongly in the principles explored in this book. I'm inviting you to take this journey with me.

I've taken stock of my day-to-day schedule, as well as my approach to observations, and I'm looking forward to shifting gears a bit after summer break.

Workaholism and inefficiency crowd out time for personal wellness, transformational leadership, and (of course) family and balance.[5]

Our journey begins with one of the most counterintuitive recommendations in this book, pushing against a contemporary leadership trend.

It's time to close that open door.

---

[5] Cue Harry Chapin's "Cat's in the Cradle."

Questions for Discussion

How do you currently distinguish between being "busy" and being "productive" in your own work life?

What are some early warning signs you personally experience when you're approaching burnout?

How visible are you in your professional community (classrooms, team meetings, informal conversations)?

If you completed the value-based diagram today, what would land in your "highest priority" tier?

1

CLOSING THE OPEN DOOR

SETTING BOUNDARIES WITH OFFICE TIME

When I first started as an administrator over two decades ago, I inherited the worst kind of open-door situation. At the time, my office was the location for the intercom system and the one window AC unit that was meant to cover my office, the adjoining administrative and receptionist area, and the nurse's station.[6]

I still remember one awkward afternoon when I was visiting with a middle school student and his parents, discussing the consequences for his recess behavior.

I suspected the parents would disagree with the decision, judging by their body language. However, before either of us could speak, my receptionist popped in to contact a teacher through the intercom. As the family and I sat in awkward pause, she repeated the teacher's name twice more in a louder voice, trying to compete with the noise of an active classroom.

---

[6] I prefer warm environments, but often I would come back from observations to find my office cold enough to store beef because it needed to serve such a large administrative space.

"We need Alex to come to the office to pick up his lunch!" my receptionist said, her voice raised. She repeated herself when it didn't appear the teacher had heard the request over the cacophony of her class activity.

Finally, the receptionist slipped out of the office, returning me and the family to the tense situation, as if we'd just paused for a commercial break. Apparently, this had been standard practice before I'd taken the position.

"So …" I began, turning back to the on-edge family. "As I just explained …"

An expansion and remodel project over the next couple of years solved my problem, and I hope that most principals have better offices than I did.[7]

Open-door policies, as they developed in the mid-20th century, originated as a feature of more participatory and transparent leadership styles.

In some cases, business leaders took the practice to such an extreme as to actually require the removal of office doors or the placement of executive desks in open spaces, with conference rooms reserved for private conversations.

Before beginning work on this book, I explored ideas for the following chapters through a short essay on efficiency that I wrote and published in a Facebook educators' group. In the essay, I presented three suggestions for overwhelmed

[7] I also got a new desk, as my previous one was at a roughly 10° angle (yes, I measured). When I would put a pencil down, it would begin rolling toward the left edge of my workspace!

administrators, including my rejection of open-door policies.

In general, the response was positive. As a bonus, I picked up great ideas from other masters of efficiency who chimed in.

However, one commenter pushed back, arguing that an open-door policy was essential to a strong culture. He wrote that he wanted his teachers, students, and parents to know he was always available. Other work would come second to their immediate needs.

While my Facebook friend and I disagreed on the merits of open-door policies, I very much appreciated his rationale of wanting to be present and attentive to the needs of his community.

While some readers, like this commenter, may feel they have successfully implemented an open-door approach, I maintain that the idea is based on a flawed underlying assumption—that the office should be the place where one would most likely find the building principal.

PRINCIPLE #1 – Inside the office is often where tasks are completed. Outside the office is where the organization's mission is fulfilled.

In this chapter, we will explore some of the ways that being too accessible in the office can sabotage culture and inhibit transformational leadership.

Following that, the chapter will present alternatives to an open-door approach, as well as suggestions on how to introduce such a change to your team.

How Open-Door Policies Can Sabotage Culture

One of my favorite books on leadership is Will Guirdara's *Unreasonable Hospitality*. Among the notes I made while reading the book is Guirdara's observation that, "in too many organizations, the people at the top have all the authority and none of the information, while the people on the front line have all the information and none of the authority."

In theory, an open-door policy seems to be a solution to disconnected management. In reality, such a leadership style can potentially disrupt the culture outside the office and the efficiency within it.

Revolving Doors – As with most school leaders, I hope to establish a reputation of accessibility and availability. However, an open-door policy can also send a message that the principal's role is to resolve every issue, big or small.

Open-door policies undermine the organizational structure and favor squeaky wheels among the team.

Should teachers, parents, or students develop such a perception, it might increase dependency on the principal as primary problem solver. If the principal's office is the path of least resistance for every issue, then *every issue* will end up at the principal's office.

Chains of Communication – School systems and other organizations typically have chains of communication that involve team leaders, department chairs, and directors as first steps before upper management. Not only can an open-door policy increase dependency on the principal, but it often undermines structures that emphasize subsidiarity.

One theory for the emergence of open-door policies posits that the strategy is a way for management to undermine the role of unions within their organization. The website for the International Union, United Automobile, Aerospace and Agricultural Implement Workers of America (UAW) argues that an "'open-door' policy means the employer will listen to you ... and then do whatever he or she wants."[v]

Whether or not you work in a school system with a strong union presence is beside the point. Open-door policies can undermine the chain of communication within school programs and undermine attempts to resolve issues at the most local level.

Teachers may bypass the IT department for their tech issues. Parents or students who request a meeting with the principal are often circumventing a conversation with the teacher that might have otherwise cleared up the issue. One team member might race to the administrative offices in order to be the first voice in the principal's ear regarding a staff conflict.

A proper organizational structure is key to ensuring the most efficient and effective response to problems or ideas. Even this process should support problem-solving and self-sufficiency, two traits that strong school teams rely on.

Squeaky Wheel Syndrome – Another inherent flaw with open-door policies, absent of any other outreach methods, is the passive nature of such leadership. An open-door assumes that those who have concerns or questions will decide to voluntarily approach school leadership.

It can seem intuitive to leaders that employees will feel comfortable coming to them with questions or concerns. After all, those of us who pursued management roles generally feel comfortable with self-advocation and with inserting ourselves into the conversation.

However, while principals may hope that all members of the school team feel comfortable bringing concerns or ideas to the boss's office, it is often the more vocal or assertive types who come knocking at the office door.

In a 2020 survey of around 6,000 professionals, fewer than 40% of the respondents felt comfortable speaking up on most issues, while 20% did not feel comfortable speaking up at all in the workplace.[vi]

Think about your own team, especially if you have a larger staff. If you were to take a roster of all of your employees, how many have approached you in your office over the last year? Of those who haven't, is it reasonable to assume they have no concerns or suggestions?

Beyond the obvious risk of stifling other voices, catering to the frequent flyers risks mixing roles and diluting the principal's authority. Staff may feel they have a personal route to push for exceptions, which can complicate policy enforcement and create perceptions of favoritism.

Whether or not one maintains an open-door policy, opportunities, and procedures need to be in place that will ensure that the perspective of all stakeholders is represented in administrative actions and key decisions.

Focusing on the Negative – If open-door policies cater to the squeaky wheels, then it would follow that such an approach only works for addressing complaints or concerns.

However, building a positive culture means seeking out the good news within an organization.

I remember a recent conversation with a teacher during which I pointed out an innovated practice that was happening in her classroom. She shared with me that she'd gotten the idea from a colleague that she had observed on her plan period.

More than likely, the teacher would not otherwise have sought me out in my office to talk about this collaboration victory, but it revealed two sparks of excellence within my team—both the teacher who first modeled the best practice and the one who used her valuable plan non-instructional time for personal growth.

The Toll of Divided Attention – Chapter two will explore the folly of multitasking. Spoiler alert—our brains aren't programmed that way, and fewer than 3% of individuals are able to multitask without decreased performance in either area.[vii] I'm pretty sure I'm among that elite group. As I chapter this write, I'm also kidding my help with homework.[8]

While I do not practice an open-door policy, I generally won't turn away those infrequent instances when someone does seek me out in person. Knowing my leadership preferences, anyone who does hunt me down in the office probably has a serious or urgent matter to discuss.

---

[8] Yes, I know you caught that, clever you! We'll discuss multitasking a bit more in chapter two.

But this doesn't mean that the timing of surprise office pop-in is ideal.

Earlier this year, a teacher popped in to ask about an administrative calendar decision. Because the conversation interrupted an urgent matter, I had allowed some frustration to show through in my tone. I reminded myself that principals should strive to model professional behavior and tone, and I apologized as a way to reset the conversation.

When individuals are confronted or challenged, alarms often sound in the amygdala, the part of the brain that responds to emotions, particular fear and anxiety. Our minds slip into fight-or-flight mode. We are more prone to react to what another says than to internalize and consider it.

> **"When people talk, listen completely. Most people never listen."**
> **-Ernest Hemingway**

Professionals should be psychologically mature enough to resist such a reaction. But when our work is interrupted, our minds often do not have time to reflect objectively.

When I do have to be in my office, I explain to others, I have matters that are urgent and need my full attention. We'll explore this more in the next chapter on time blocking.

But when visitors interrupt my focus on critical matters, I struggle with pulling my attention away from whatever had sucked me back into my office in the first place.[9]

"When you stop by my office," I tell my team, "you're likely to catch me hyper-focused on a deadline or in the middle of a complicated task. If I don't have time to reset my thoughts, there's a good risk that my preoccupied brain is probably only giving you a fraction of the attention you deserve."

Principals are tasked with steering the school's vision, not managing each question or complaint in real time. Being available is essential, but an effective leader knows that setting boundaries, far from closing people off, actually creates space for more focused work with their teams.

The Alternative: An Open-Calendar Policy

At my first staff meeting with the team I currently serve, I discussed my dislike of open-door approaches.

"It isn't that I want to limit my availability to you. Exactly the opposite," I assured them after briefly touching preference for an *open-calendar* approach. "I'll be visible in the halls and popping by your classrooms often. But when you need to speak with me, I want to be available and fully attentive.

"When you schedule the meeting with me," I continued, "I can make sure that nothing interrupts our time together and that I'm focused solely on your concern."

My son recently appeared in his grade school's adaptation

---

[9] This is also why I always do post-observation conferences the day *after* I've visited a classroom. I don't think it is fair to interrupt a teacher's plan period without sufficient notice.

of *The Wizard of Oz* as a hyperactive, mischievous monkey.[10]

Reflecting on the storyline, it seems that transformative leaders should strive to be more like Glenda the Good Witch, than the Wizard.

The Great and Powerful Oz had an open-door policy. But Dorothy and her crew had to, first, muster the courage to visit him.

They then needed to make the journey.

Finally, they got to encounter the Wizard at a time when he was obviously not prepared to entertain their requests. "Come back tomorrow," he told them, even after they had fulfilled his request to retrieve the Wicked Witch's broom.

Glenda the Good Witch, on the other hand, didn't wait for Dorothy or her three friends to seek her out. She met Dorothy where she was, offering support and helping the misplaced Kansan realize that the answer to her dilemma had been within her all along.

Earlier in this chapter, I argued that open-door policies can undermine the proper chains of command within an organization. It would be a fair criticism to suggest the same could happen with an open-calendar approach.

Yes, an open-calendar approach can be abused, but when individuals catch a principal off guard by popping by the office, the conversation is often impulsive.

In situations that involve a conflict or disruption, the

---

10 #typecasting

Teachers generally do not use calendars the way administrators do. A teacher's schedule is often regimented by the bell system.

For this reason, some on your team may not know *how* to set up meetings on a calendar. When establishing an open-calendar norm, it is important to take time at a staff meeting to display a digital calendar and demonstrate the steps in setting up a meeting with others.

individual requesting the meeting hasn't had time to process the occurrence, and the leader is put into a reaction mindset.

Teachers and other staff *should* have the principal's ear, but when meetings are scheduled, the principal can enter the conversation prepared to listen actively and give guidance that respects the appropriate paths of resolution.

Also, by setting up a meeting ahead of time, the staff member gives you a heads up so that you can do any preliminary preparation to make sure you're able to participate fully in the conversation.

Asking for meetings to be scheduled in advance also cuts down on knee-jerk meetings based more on reaction and emotion. Meetings scheduled even an hour into the future also give individuals time to reflect and cool down when some conflict is at stake. Further, the act of pulling up a calendar and scheduling a meeting is a much more intentional act than darting to the principal's office. Intentionality is the antidote for impulsivity.

Sometimes, of course, matters are so urgent that scheduling a meeting in advance is not an option. A teacher's spouse needs her to head home. An encounter with an angry parent calls for an immediate and compassionate ear. A major classroom fail calls for prompt reassurance and guidance.

"In instances like these," explain to your team, "I need to be available for you. You can either text me or have someone in the office hunt me down."

Other Strategies for Visibility and Availability

Even the approach of scheduling meetings is a relatively passive strategy for stakeholder feedback. By using check-in meetings and other intentional principal-staff interactions as a complement to an open-door policy, principals can more fully democratize the communication process, making sure that others beyond the squeaky wheels are heard.

Other types of lower-urgency moments also allow leaders to, like Glenda the Good Witch, guide individuals to discover their inherent ability to overcome challenges.

Regular Check-In Meetings – Scheduling short, regular one-on-one conversations or team check-ins can be a game-changer. These meetings are intentional time set aside for staff to raise issues, discuss challenges, and share updates. They help avoid the random walk-ins and keep conversations focused.

Plus, with these regular touchpoints, leaders are better able to track ongoing projects and support team member needs in a more systematic way. For staff, it creates a clear opportunity to discuss issues rather than hoping to catch a principal in passing.

Proactive Walkthroughs and Pop-Ins – Chapter eight's discussion of effective observations and feedback will emphasize the benefits of short, frequent observations, followed by reflective conversations.

In addition to instructional leadership, this approach also gives dedicated face time to teachers, especially when principals occasionally ask about the teacher's well-being or feedback.

Setting up clear communication channels helps staff know appropriate ways to express different ideas or concerns.

These visits allow for quick conversations that don't derail the day and often make teachers feel seen and supported without having to seek out an administrator.

Scheduled "Pulse" Meetings – Grouping teachers or staff into small "pulse" meeting groups that gather bi-weekly or monthly can be another effective alternative.

Collective feedback has a powerful amplification effect when team members begin building off of one another's ideas.

Pulse meetings are also a valuable way to keep a finger on, well, the *pulse* of the school without tackling each issue in isolation.

And since you're guiding the meeting, you can steer conversations in ways that stay focused and constructive.

Obviously, group meetings will not curb individual or

private concerns that might be brought to your office, but often staff appreciate opportunities to be heard, especially when leaders show investment in constructive concerns or suggestions.

Setting Boundaries for Interruptions

As mentioned earlier in this chapter, there will always be situations that require an immediate response, but setting some basic ground rules can help you manage these moments.

Dr. Justin Baeder, director of *The Principal Center*, suggests that by establishing low walls of accessibility, principals can emphasize the importance of their role as active coaches among the team.[viii]

Baeder suggests categorizing professional issues into four categories:

- Safety matters, such as major discipline issues, call for an immediate **interruption** of the principal's schedule.

- For some urgent matters, Baeder suggests having office staff **consult** with the principal.

- In some cases, while the matter must be handled by administration, such as a low-level discipline issue, office staff can simply **inform** the principal by email or when she returns to the office.

- Finally, office staff can responsibly **handle** many issues, though these team members and the principal should discuss what issues should be **documented** and in what manner.

Take a moment to reflect on Baeder's advice. In the

organizational chart below, jot down some issues you regularly deal with in your professional role.

Place these in the column that best represents the "low wall" that would help protect your time as a leader of instruction and culture.

Low Wall Responses			
Interrupt	**Consult**	**Inform**	**Handle**

By helping office personnel and other staff understand the difference between emergencies and less urgent matters, principals encourage good time stewardship while also building self-reliance among the team.[11]

As principals, our presence matters, but an intentional

[11] Having a friendly, but confident and competent administrative assistant is a treasure beyond value. In addition to being a delegate for many administrative tasks, this individual is the gatekeeper that allows you to major on the majors in your instructional leadership role.

approach to being accessible ensures that when staff do connect with us, it's in a way that's focused, impactful, and geared toward growth for everyone.

However, even when leaders articulated a clear line between office work and the more important mission within classrooms and hallways, challenges remain. Foremost among those distinctions is the mental clutter of an over-populating to-do list. Chapter two explores value-based scheduling and the benefits of time blocking.

- Open-door policies can create dependency, disrupt focus, and suggest favoritism.
- An open-calendar policy is a good alternative to ensure focused and intentional conversations.
- Other alternatives include structured office hours, regular check-ins, pulse meetings, and proactive walkthroughs.
- Effective leadership requires intentional accessibility and reasonable boundaries.

Questions for Discussion

How has an open-door policy helped or hindered your leadership effectiveness in the past?

In what ways could an open-calendar policy create a stronger, more intentional culture of communication in your organization?

How do you currently balance urgent interruptions versus scheduled priorities, and where do you see room for improvement?

What systems do you have in place (or could put in place) to make sure all voices—not just the "squeaky wheels"—are heard?

2

TO-DO OR NOT TO-DO?

TIME BLOCKING

In Lewis Carroll's *Through the Looking-Glass*, Alice finds herself in a disorienting world, the rules of which are often the mirror-opposite of her own.

Deep in the story, as she runs alongside the Red Queen, Alice realizes she's remained in the same spot. The Red Queen explains, matter-of-factly, "Now, here, you see, it takes all the running you can do to keep in the same place."

This logic may feel eerily familiar to anyone buried under a mountain of to-do lists. We move frantically from task to task, answering emails, sitting in meetings, and putting out small fires, all in hopes of feeling caught up.

To-do lists are the scheduling equivalent of an open-door policy—seemingly helpful, but often unfocused. The school day becomes an experiment in motion without direction.

Only, as the dismissal bell sounds, we realize that—like Alice—we've been running all this time just to stay in the same place. To make real progress, we need more than motion—we need purpose.

PRINCIPLE #2 – Move from defining your purpose by a list of tasks to prioritizing your responsibilities according to mission.

The guidance in chapter one can help principals get out from the office and into a pursuit of mission. This chapter continues that discussion by exploring how professionals can use time blocking as a way to pry from beneath the weight of our complex roles.

The Problems with To-Do Lists

In her article "A Workaholic's Guide to Reclaiming Your Life," author Malissa Clark argues that research shows "only a weak correlation between number of hours worked and problematic 'overwork' or workaholism."[ix]

Don't let your schedule define your priorities. Rather, your priorities should define your schedule.

Clark continues on to define workaholism as the inability to keep one's thoughts of work from disrupting a healthy work-life balance.

When I have a lot going on and my brain kicks into overdrive, I will sometimes wake in the middle of the night, remembering something I need or want to do.

Unless I write these thoughts down immediately, I will toss and turn for the next hour.

Jotting down any upcoming tasks and deadlines is helpful and can relieve overload anxiety. But tackling the list in arbitrary order usually leads to inefficiency.[12]

To-do lists give the impression of solving a problem. By listing our tasks and responsibilities on a piece of paper, we feel the impossible load upon our shoulders is conquered. The brain gets a hit of dopamine, and we feel like we've accomplished something—even if we haven't yet acted.

There's nothing wrong with creating a to-do list as an initial step in reckoning with our responsibilities and deadlines, but this approach often decreases our overall efficiency and effectiveness. This is because there are fundamental flaws with a to-do list approach.

First, to-do lists fail to consider the urgency or importance of items on the list, as well as the resources and time needed to address them.

As an analogy, making a list of one's debts is a great way to begin constructing a budget. However, deciding which debts to tackle depends on many factors. Which have the highest interest rates? Which can be eliminated quickly?

Second, to-do lists do not consider the schedules of collaborators.

For instance, early in second semester, our team needs to

---

[12] So, true story. This guy I know (not me) was finishing his dissertation on teacher evaluations. ~~My~~ His brain woke him around two in the morning with the crazy idea to write the acknowledgements in the form of a villanelle, one of the most restrictive and, therefore, difficult poems to write. He couldn't go to sleep until, yes, he spent two hours working out the poem. What a nut ...

start discussing graduation and other end-of-year activities. This will take a significant chunk of time when several stakeholders are available.

Finally, to-do lists increase one's mental load and encourage the unproductive practice of multitasking.

Author Seth Godin's book *This is Strategy* coaches readers into making better decisions and effecting change. Godin maintains that "you don't need more time in your day. You need to decide."[x]

The stress of trying to accomplish every task leads to the temptation to actually attempt to do it all *right now*! This is especially true time is not scheduled for key items. One task bleeds into another or spills over into the next day.

As I started this chapter, I thought about one of my sons, who struggles with inattentive ADHD. With the right strategies, an overactive brain can enhance creativity, adaptability, and intuition.

However, ADHD can also be an obstacle to organization and productivity, especially for young people in classrooms that are not set up for those of us whose brains operate like a popcorn machine.

A to-do list mirrors the way my son's mind often works—everything feels urgent, and nothing gets sorted.

As a result, many professionals—even those with calmer neural networks—attempt to multitask when faced with an overload of responsibilities.

Some forms of multi-tasking are possible and productive.

For instance, going for a walk increases cognitive function and can enhance creative thought. One can typically think and walk at the same time.

But this is a rare type of multitasking in which one task is chosen to augment another. Walking is a perfunctory act that requires little conscious coordination, but which gets the blood flowing, delivering more oxygen to the muscles and brain.

To-do lists increase one's mental load and encourage the unhealthy and unproductive practice of multitasking.

Generally speaking, however, research has established that splitting our attention between two focused tasks weakens both working memory and long-term retention.[xi]

As expressed well in a quote attributed to Alexander Graham Bell, "Concentrate all your thoughts upon the work at hand. The sun's rays do not burn until brought to a focus."

Even jumping quickly from one item to another on a list drains focus and reduces efficiency through task-switch cost.

Multitasking may give the appearance of accomplishing more, but a shotgun approach to one's to-do list typically allows only a shallow amount of cognitive function to each task. It prevents deep and sustained engagement.

Revisiting a Value-Based Mindset

In the introduction, we used a trapezoidal graphic

organizer to categorize our tasks and responsibilities. The purpose of that exercise was to think about our responsibilities at a superficial level, as I didn't define the criteria any more specifically than value-based.

In this chapter, we're going to develop this list further by using the Eisenhower Matrix, a popular graphic organizer for evaluating the priority of one's responsibilities and challenges based on importance and urgency.

The Eisenhower Matrix

	High Urgency	Low Urgency
High Importance	• Observations • Follow-up Conversations • Teach Class	• Administrative Meetings • Diocesan paperwork • Weekly tactical meetings • Hiring interviews • Plan in-service • Data analysis
Low Importance	• Supervision • Dismissal • Tackling Email • Hallway visibility	• Mail • Low-level student discipline • Student letters of recommendation • Community commitments • Thank-you notes

The organizer above lists a few of my responsibilities. Some are pulled from the exercise in the introduction, while others are items that are on my plate right now.

In later chapters, I'll interact with the Eisenhower Matrix[13] a bit more as we explore the extent to which additional strategies increase efficiency.

The top and bottom rows separate items by importance, while the left and right columns designate urgency.

The top, left corner of your grid should include those items that are nonnegotiable and urgent.

Thinking in terms of urgency and importance helps shift us from vague ideas of value to clear prioritization. It's a step toward preventing Kim Marshall's *hyperactive superficial principal syndrome.*

Sometimes a task like responding to emails or supervising a hallway *is* more important than completing a classroom observation.

Every decision a principal makes about how to use time and energy is value-based, but value must be specific to context.

On the following page, you can complete your own matrix. Our lists won't be exhaustive, and this isn't an exercise you need to complete every day or week.

This is just a way to start training our brains to see tasks

---

[13] Curious readers may find interesting to know that the Eisenhower Matrix is named, of course, for the 1999 biopic starring Keanu Reeves in the title role during the 34th president's younger days as a cyberpunk ninja guy.

in light of the bigger scope of our roles.

The Eisenhower Matrix

High Urgency / High Importance	Low Urgency / High Importance
High Urgency / Low Importance	**Low Urgency / Low Importance**

Having at least an abstract understanding of the urgency and importance of your tasks now allows us to move from the to-do list method used by our primitive ancestors and into the exciting world of … *time blocking.*

Time Blocking – An Alternative to Multi-Tasking

We organize our physical spaces. Except for that gallimaufry drawer in the kitchen, cabinets and shelves have their purpose. Even if our *feng shui* isn't calibrated, some visceral instinct doesn't let us store tax documents with our pet supplies.

Just like our offices and homes, our schedule should be filled with purpose. *Time-blocking* is a strategy that minimizes distractions and encourages focus.[14]

Segmenting the day into dedicated tasks helps leaders weigh the importance and urgency of a task, outlining a clear plan for one's day.

By mapping out one's schedule in advance, a principal can ensure the right tasks get the time they deserve. Each block in the schedule has a dedicated purpose and an allotment of time appropriate to the task, whether one's goal is to complete the item or make significant progress.

I don't finalize each day's schedule until the night before or early that morning. This leaves room for flexibility. This allows gaps in my schedule for appointments in the days ahead if team members need to meet.

Blocks can be assigned to future days and weeks as placeholders. For instance, I need to catch up on thank-you notes this week, so I might insert a block for this later in the week. The time can always be adjusted as my week takes shape.

As I look over my earlier to-do list, I can see some non-negotiables that I need to wrap up early in the week before I head out of state on Tuesday and Wednesday. For those items, I've scheduled brief check-in meetings with the administrative

---

14 "Some folks say I take calendar management too seriously. But if color-coding your lunch break and setting a five-minute buffer for chewing isn't peak efficiency, I don't know what is." -Gordon H. Sputtle, CPA, MBA

team at points when each of our calendars shows availability.

As mentioned, I am teaching a class this year, so that block is solidly in place as a recurring commitment.

8 AM
Administrative Check-In
9 AM
Creative Writing
8:50 – 9:50am
10 AM
Email, 9:50am
11 AM
Lunch Supervision
10:40 – 11:40am
12 PM
Observations
11:45am – 12:45pm
1 PM
Follow-Up Conversation
12:45 – 1:45pm
2 PM
Work on Calendar
1:45 – 2:45pm
3 PM

The time I schedule for follow-ups generally aligns with the planning period of teachers I observed the previous day, though I might try to tuck these in before or after school if it works better for the teacher.

I've also scheduled time tomorrow for email and calendar updates.

Typically, many of the blocks in my schedule are slightly larger than I suspect will be necessary, an intentional overestimation in case I underestimate a task's complexity.

Ensuring Availability

In school settings, most of the faculty and staff are on fixed schedules, with availability pre-determined by class schedules. While I do sometimes leave buffer gaps in my schedule, it's rare that my available times line up with the plan period of a teacher who needs to discuss something.

The better practice, I've found, is to invite team members to schedule at least a day ahead of time, but to let them know

Time blocking is especially useful for ensuring teacher observations take place at a variety of times. One strategy is to put all observations within cycles of observations at the same general time of day, choosing different times of the day each cycle.

This ensures both continuity among teachers and a greater variety of observation times feeding into the big picture of what is happening in each teacher's classroom.

that *almost* anything on my schedule can be put to the side for a sufficiently urgent matter.

Schools are far from predictable. But while a principal should always be ready to move items around for unexpected emergencies, remember to utilize those low walls from chapter one as a way to protect your time for important items.

Adjusting to Time Blocking

Despite just having written a chapter about time blocking, I'll admit that I don't execute the practice perfectly, and that's okay.

As with any suggestion in this book, time blocking can be effective, even if implemented gradually.

Everything is gradual, a point I will reiterate with the conclusion's focus on maintaining a work-life balance. When I'm working on a dedicated task, my mind still whispers temptations to get off task.

Did that parent respond to my email?

Wait, is it time to fill out FAFSA for Bryce?

Are they still working on a reboot of Police Academy*?*

Even disciplined minds know there is no perfectly-planned day in school settings. Principals are often the problem-solvers for many unexpected crises. Tech failures. Heated phone call. Morning detention with the loyalty club members.

As Robert Burns wrote, "The best-laid plans o' mice an' principals are often interrupted by first-grade boys having distance contests at the urinals."

Or something like that. It's been a while since I read Burns.

But an altered plan is better than no plan at all. Thinking about your own tasks and responsibilities, what items are non-negotiable?

Which are time-sensitive?

Which cans do you just keep kicking down the road?

Time blocking isn't just about efficiency. As with a move away from open-door policies, value-based scheduling is an alignment of the professional day with vision and values.

Acting with intentionality ensures that time and attention can be given to what matters most: instruction and culture.

- Traditional to-do lists lack prioritization and encourage multitasking, leading to inefficiency and stress.
- Tasks should be assessed for urgency and importance to ensure time and energy are allocated effectively.
- Time blocking promotes focus, structure, and intentionality.
- Allow room in schedules for urgent matters, unexpected interruptions, and adjustments without derailing priorities.
- Intentional scheduling aligns time with values and priorities, enabling leaders to focus on high-impact activities like coaching and cultural transformation.

Questions for Discussion

How does your current method of organizing tasks (to-do lists, mental notes, etc.) help or hinder your true priorities as a leader?

In what ways could time blocking immediately improve your focus and reduce your sense of overwhelm?

What specific challenges might you face when trying to transition from multitasking to focused time blocking?

Reflecting on your leadership values, what transformational activities (like coaching or culture-building) deserve their own protected time blocks on your calendar?

3

BATTLING THE HYDRA

EMBRACING AN INBOX-ZERO MINDSET

In the 2003 movie *Bruce Almighty*, God has loaned his omnipotence to the titular character as a lesson in humility.

In one scene, Bruce opens his *Yahweh! Insta-Prayer* window to find a million-and-a-half petitions in his inbox. By the time he had answered them all, new requests had arrived. Over three million of them.

When email emerged in the early 1970s and was later introduced to a more widespread user base, the tool promised to increase efficiency by streamlining communications.

As opposed to meetings and phone calls, the asynchronous nature of email allowed both flexibility and convenience. Send a message whenever you want. Reply when it suits you.

In reality, the Faustian promises of efficiency through email cluttered our inboxes with spam, including Uncle Ron's daily joke forward and offers of financial freedom from exiled Nigerian royalty.

As if that kind of clutter wasn't enough, the immediacy of

email (and eventually text) added a sense of urgency to work, especially when senders discovered how to use the priority flag and the exclamation mark.

Email can be a useful tool—but not always an efficient one. This is because many have lost a sense of boundaries in professional communications. Emails tend to be too long, too frequent, and too urgent.

The final chapter in this book will look at balance, and email is the perfect case study of how efficiency is only healthy to the extent that professionals do not allow it to define the narrative of one's day.

PRINCIPLE #3 – Email and other tools of efficiency, if not managed well, threaten to overwhelm leaders and undermine the organization's mission.

This chapter and the next explore how leaders can reestablish boundaries to restore both efficiency and sanity.

The Inbox-Zero Mindset

Some of you took a quick peek at your inbox after the *Bruce Almighty* intro. Others were afraid to look. For some readers, the number of messages in their inbox—never deleted or sorted into folders—might be in the thousands.

Reclaiming our inbox is about more than practical efficiency. As with a daunting to-do list, a cluttered wasteland

of received messages can take a psychological toll on professionals.

A 2024 survey of over 1,000 professionals revealed that nearly 80% have experienced dread over opening their work inbox, and nearly 60% have this reaction regularly.[xii] Almost three-quarters of respondents reported that burnout affected their communications with loved ones.

Attacking a cluttered inbox can feel like a battle with the mythical hydra, the creature that grew two new heads for each one that a hero would decapitate. So, consider this your invitation into the exclusive *inbox-zero* club. The picture above is a screenshot of my phone earlier today. I have to show that to Bruno, the bouncer, to get into the club lounge.

Striving for an empty inbox will discipline both you and your inbox, even if it sometimes feels like a Sisyphean struggle.

But for your own sanity, remember that the goal is to *strive for* zero. I don't advise setting a hard mandate for yourself that the inbox be near empty all the time or even at the end of your workday.

The suggestions in this chapter are about developing a discipline that keeps your electronic communications in check.

As the philosopher and historian Will Durant wrote,

"Excellence is not an act, but a habit."[15]

This chapter is about reminding yourself that email is your servant, not the other way around. The tips you will find in the next few sections are intended to reduce the time you spend with email and the stress that it brings to your professional life.

Delete, Delegate, Respond, and Defer

For every email you receive, one of four possible actions are appropriate: delete, delegate, respond, and defer.[16]

Delete – Of the nearly 350 billion emails sent every day in 2023, just under half of them were spam.[xiii] With the rise of generative AI, that number has likely increased substantially by the time you read this chapter.[17]

Strong filters take care of most unwanted spam, but much of it still slips through. For principals, much of this clutter comes from solicitors who either purchased your address from email harvesters or got it when you registered to win a cooler at that convention booth.

Either way, deleting the email only takes care of the problem today. If an easy one-button *unsubscribe* option appears, click it (and then delete).

Otherwise, any decent email platform offers the option to

---

[15] On the Saturday morning that I do my first read-through revision, I have three messages since cleaning out my inbox the day before. They'll wait until Monday.
[16] To my OCD friends, I'm sorry I couldn't come up with a good "d" synonym for *respond*. Yes, it bothers me, too.
[17] Yes, it turns out that Skynet never intended to subjugate us with cyborgs, but with hundreds of spammy emails a day promising to transform our school culture and supercharge instruction.

block senders or mark their messages as spam before deleting. Yes, this is an extra step, but one that pays dividends down the road, though it may be months before the benefits are obvious.

Deleting an email solves today's problem. But clicking 'unsubscribe' or blocking senders addresses—while a slow burn—is an investment today that pays dividends down the road.

Even beyond spam, most other emails don't deserve more than a quick tap of the delete key. As tempting as it may feel, you *probably* shouldn't mark the Monday superintendent's message as spam, but most of what you get from the central office is probably informational only.[18]

Not every email needs a response. Especially among generations who grew up before the proliferation of electronic communications, it seems rude not to reply in some way.

Got it!

I'll be there!

Thanks!

But, unless the sender requests a response (either directly or implicitly), just do put that finger over the delete button. Deep breath and … boom!

I began with the section on deletion because it provides instant gratification. When I feel ready to collapse inside because I see 130 emails waiting for my attention, scrolling

---

[18] But these messages *can* be delegated to an administrative assistant to read and manage. A good assistant will let you know what you need from those messages.

through and deleting the fluff often reduces that number to 40ish that actually require some action on my part. Your mileage may vary.

Administrators often find themselves with pockets of dead time throughout the day. Waiting for a supervision duty, filling my truck with gas, feigning attention at district meetings. Most settings allow swipe deletes, which I've found to be an easy way to reduce my inbox when I've got five minutes to spare in transition.

While not quite a deletion, *filing* emails achieves the same purpose. I would have included filing in the acronym, but now look how sloppy it's getting: DFDRD.

Many people leave too many emails in their inbox simply because the messages might be important for later retrieval.

But these emails can be stored in folders or tagged with appropriate labels. Examples of folders I have used include those set up for emails related to personnel matters, travel expenses, and projects I am working on.

Tagging emails or setting them to circle back at a later date reduces professional stress by ensuring accountability.

The point is to get them out of the inbox. Out of sight, out of mind, and out of the way as you conquer your workday.

Delegate – Those who do not understand the role of a principal or other organizational leader often view that individual as the one-stop fix-it person. Chapter seven discusses delegation in more detail, but this section will look at some helpful strategies for delegating effectively while clearing out the inbox.

While simply forwarding the email to an administrative assistant or team member is often sufficient, I prefer another approach for many emails.

By replying to the original sender and cc'ing the team member to whom I'm delegating, I can assure the sender that I've given the matter my attention while reinforcing the chain of responsibilities in the school:

> **Message:** Good morning, Mrs. Paden. Thanks for reaching out. I've cc'd your daughter's counselor. She's on top of the NHS requirements and will be able to give you the best guidance on this. Thanks for your partnership!

However, school systems are complicated and often messy organizations. It's easy for important matters to slip between the cracks and reflect poorly upon the principal and the team member responsible for the task.

While email read receipts can be helpful, these often have shortcomings, such as being dependent on the recipient to authorize the receipt. Read receipts also do not ensure that action is taken after an email is opened and read.

Many programs now allow emails to be scheduled for later follow-up. The school I am currently at uses Gmail, which doesn't currently allow for this. But various extensions exist that can add functionality.

I use the paid version of an add-on called *Boomerang for*

Gmail to ensure my delegated task is completed. The follow-up ensures that the message returns to my inbox so I can confirm it's been handled.

The follow-up can be set to return to one's index if the recipient fails to reply to or even open the message. Using the follow-up feature allows me to delegate and forget:

> **Subject:** Retreat Lunch
>
> **Message:** Greg, I just realized that we need to get catering quotes for next month's retreat lunch. If you'll get some pricing, I'll set this email to circle back next week, and we can look over the options you find at our Friday meeting.

Once I've sent this message, I can stop worrying about the lunch. Greg's got it. But on the off-chance his schedule gets overloaded, I set the email to circle back the day before our meeting "regardless" as a reminder to check in with him.

For readers whose email programs do not have a useful follow-up option, a good alternative is to just set calendar reminders to circle back on delegated tasks.[19]

Respond – A later section of this chapter will discuss effective email responses, but as a general guideline, emails should be as short as possible without compromising the tone or message. Once the response has been sent, the original email can be deleted or filed away.

---

[19] Boomerang has a free version with limited uses, but I've found the tool helpful enough to spring for the paid license. Microsoft allows users to tag emails to remind the sender or recipients to follow up at a later date. In the **Tags** group of the **Message** tab, users can select **Follow Up**, and then select **Custom**.

Research suggests that the most effective days to send an email, in order, are Thursday, Tuesday, and Wednesday.

The most effective times tend to be 10 a.m., 9 a.m., and 8 a.m.

These are the times that most professionals have settled into their workweeks and are ready to tackle the inbox

The message delay feature can be used strategically to hit these sweet spots.

Defer – Deferring an email is essentially a delegation to your future self. To defer is not to procrastinate, which is to put off some item of work because you simply don't have the initiative to deal with it.

Rather, it is an acknowledgement that some point in the future will be a more appropriate time to handle the matter. As with the follow-up feature, most email programs allow messages to be snoozed or deferred to a later date.[20]

Early in my career, our superintendent would send out an August email with required forms for the year. While one or two of the forms were easily completed at that time, others were dependent on data collection or planning that would not take place until later in the semester. After downloading the forms appropriate to August, I could then defer the email to a

[20] And if they don't yet, they will soon. The major players in any technology are always stealing ideas from their competitors.

later date when the remaining forms could be addressed.

Just recently, I received an email from a parent with a helpful suggestion on how one of our fall events could be improved. By deferring the message to a month or so before the event, I am reminding my future self to discuss it during our planning meeting.

Other Useful Email Tools

Delaying Messages – Most email platforms now allow users to delay when a message is sent.

Sometimes I want to send an email to get a matter off my plate, but I want to respect the work/home balance of the recipient. For instance, if I realize on a Friday afternoon that I need to delegate a task to a member of my team, I can compose the message and set it to send on Monday morning.

Another use for delayed messages is to send myself timed reminders. Sometimes I'll remember a task I need to complete in the evening. Unless I get it off my mind, I'll have trouble going to sleep. I can send myself a message, delayed until the appropriate day, to address the matter.

Inbox Pause – Many email clients allow inboxes to be paused. Pause features allow automatic responses informing the sender that you will attend to emails at a later time.

I personally do not use automatic responses, however, as it creates just one more piece of mail in the sender's inbox. Because I typically check email at least twice during the workday, I feel that my responses are timely enough anyway.

Many pause settings allow for messages to bypass the pause

under certain conditions, such as a keyword in the subject line or if the email came from a sender from an approved list.

For instance, a principal might open the gate for any emails from other members of the administrative team.

Cluttered and unorganized emails are a speedbump in the search for efficiency and competency. An important email from someone who expects an action or response can easily get buried in an overloaded inbox.

While managing one's inbox is a great first step, organizational norms for communication are key.

Chapter four will discuss establishing a common communication protocol throughout the building benefits not just the principal but all of the very busy members of the school team.

- Emails often lack boundaries, are overly frequent, and feel unnecessarily urgent.
- Adopt an inbox-zero approach using four actions: delete, delegate, respond, and defer to keep emails organized and manageable.
- Use features like delayed messages, follow-ups, and pausing inboxes to streamline email handling and avoid constant interruptions.
- Establish clear communication protocols to improve efficiency and reduce clutter for both leaders and staff.

Questions for Discussion

How does the current state of your email inbox affect your daily stress levels and sense of control?

Are there times when having a cluttered inbox has caused complications or damage within the workplace?

In what ways could adopting a "delete, delegate, respond, defer" discipline immediately improve your email management?

What systems or habits do you currently have (or could create) to ensure important emails don't get lost in the clutter?

4

ALL TOGETHER NOW!

ORGANIZATIONAL COMMUNICATION BEST PRACTICES

"Dear dumbass, If you are going to …"

The morning I started this chapter, I did a quick check of my inbox and spotted an interesting email. I didn't recognize the sender's name, but the content preview showed me seven words quoted above.

Now let's be clear, I'm actually surprised I don't get three to five emails a day that start out with "Dear dumbass," but it turns out that this message was not intended for me.

The sender and I had both received a phishing email the night before. My copy of it had gone straight into the spam folder, but "James" (whom I did not know) had clicked the reply *to all* option and included each of the several dozen original recipients' responses.

"Dear dumbass," James had written, "If you are going to try to scam me, don't be stupid and show me the emails of the other 200 people you sent this to."

James made three great points all of us can take to heart:

- Don't scam people.
- Don't be a dumbass who does stupid stuff.
- Don't do a visible mass distribution to 200 random people.

The suggestions in the last chapter can be useful to any member of your team as a way of increasing efficiency and effectiveness. But this chapter, which also discusses electronic communications, goes beyond the benefits for any one individual.

Emails, texts, and other electronic communication—if not governed by clear protocols—can become a death by a thousand cuts to productivity.

The bigger problem with loose communication protocol within a building, however, is that building programs and building culture can experience set-backs due to poorly-communicated tone, information overload, and other keyboard follies.

Leaders set the tone for communication. When expectations are clear, the wheels of the whole building move faster—and with less grinding.

PRINCIPLE #4 – By establishing a team-wide norm for communication best practices, organizational leaders work toward a more finely-tuned overall system for all stakeholders.

The following sections will look at some very specific strategies and formats for communications within a professional system.

General Norms for Communication

Before discussing strategies for effective communications with their staff, principals and other organizational leaders should keep several concepts in mind.

Cultural and Generational Differences – Discussing how text tone is interpreted across the team can prevent misunderstandings and support inclusive communication.

Some individuals consider a "thumbs up" emoji to be passive aggressive, and others view periods the same way when used with few word responses (e.g., Sure. Or: Okay.).[21] Likewise, members of your team may use excessive bold or capitalized words in communications, which can come across as aggressive or expressive of anger.

Multiple exclamation marks can have the same effect, while the sender simply intended to express excitement. Individuals rarely intent these tones when drafting emails. Team discussions about how tone in text is interpreted can raise awareness of potential pitfalls.[22]

Use the Right Tool for the Job – As much as possible,

---

[21] Alas, social media has turned exclamation marks into the new period. I was recently texting with my daughter. After one of my responses, she asked why I always use a period in text. "Because it's a sentence," I answered. "Well, stop it," she responded. "It makes it look like you're in a bad mood." I was tempted to reply with a thumbs up and a period after the emoji, but due to a rare genetic defect, she was born without the ability to laugh at my jokes (and also a need to buy daily caramel-flavored cold brews—her body doesn't produce its own caramel).

[22] This is just me trying to make up for my struggle with alliteration in the last chapter. I'm sure there's a support group I should join.

text should be avoided for detailed discussions or communications. Personal texts are discoverable in legal proceedings if a they might contain any sensitive information about students or personnel. Text also makes far too easy to blur boundaries between work and home.

Clear expectations for professional communication help ensure one's efforts encounter fewer obstacles.

That said, I'm guilty of using text more than I should, but many messages that I've sent could have easily been communicated using instant messaging tools that are already part of your organization's professional communication tool. Gmail and Microsoft both provide *Chat*, an alternative that keeps communications tied to the school's domain.

Respecting Boundaries – This is an area I have had to work on as a building leader.[23] Sometimes I might find pockets of time in the evening or weekends to catch up on emails, and it seems perfectly reasonable to me that everyone else is sitting around waiting to discuss work stuff, as well.

But those aren't always ideal times for your team or parents to receive communication.

The previous chapter discussed the use of the *Send Later* features in many email programs, which allows a Sunday email

---

[23] Night owls and light sleepers will surely agree that there's a moment of connection that occurs when one sends an email at 3:00 in the morning ... *and gets a response.* You've found a kindred spirit out there.

to be scheduled to send during the next workday.

Intentionality with Tone – Tone can be successfully communicated in text. However, many individuals are not skilled enough to pull this off in delicate conversations. When in doubt, default to a phone call or an in-person visit.

While the next chapter discusses AI in length, I often advise members of my team that, if they struggle with the appropriate tone to use with a parent or colleague, they should write the email they're tempted to send, but then have a generative program like ChatGPT rewrite it in a tone of partnership. While they should always review the AI version before sending it, the tool will help them with tone and grammar.

Here is an example of an AI email revision:

Original Message:

Mrs. Smith, your knucklehead son Alex has turned in several late assignments for civics class. Right now, he is at a D, and he will probably fail if he doesn't get his act together.

Please talk with him at home about prioritizing homework over Fortnite. This is NOT a recipe for success in life!!

AI Prompt:

Rewrite this email to a parent of an 11th grade student so that the tone is positive and emphasizes partnership. Keep the response to one paragraph.

AI Revision:

Dear Mrs. Smith,

I wanted to reach out to share a quick update on Alex's progress in civics class. He's had a few late assignments recently, and his current grade is a D. I'm confident that with some renewed focus and support, he can get back on track.

I'd really appreciate it if you could check in with him at home about setting aside time for homework—we're both on Team Alex and want to help him finish the semester strong. Please don't hesitate to reach out if you'd like to talk through any strategies together.[24]

Using AI to help in email or in other areas of professional work is a conversation in and of itself. In the next chapter, we will explore the power of AI to improve administrator efficiency, including best practices, ethics, and responsible use.

Clarity and Conciseness – When drafting emails and texts, be more Hemingway than Faulkner.[25] I was recently humbled when, on a recent feedback survey, a couple of team members commented that it was sometimes hard to locate information in my weekly newsletter.

Professional communication is generally intended to communicate information directly and efficiently. Taking the

---

[24] For this particular issue, I'd strongly suggest a phone call to Jamie's parents would have been the most powerful means of initiating this conversation.

[25] Hemingway was short and to the point. Faulkner's *Absalom, Absalom!* contains a sentence with 1,288 words.

survey feedback to heart, I brainstormed with my administrative assistant about how to improve the newsletter. Then, I delegated it to her!

The improvements she brought to the newsletter, including color-coding and greater brevity, were perfect.[26]

I shouldn't have been doing the newsletter anyway. It was one of my last holdouts in the process of delegating my tasks away. Part of that process is realizing when others can do something for you, but also when they can do it better than you.

Workplace Emails

Remember our friend James? His response to a phishing email was my lead for this chapter. Unfortunately for James, the *dumbass* who sent that email was probably an automated program that couldn't care less about James's response.

But the rest of us got to see it, because our keyboard vigilante James decided to reply *to all* of the recipients, including me. Of the workplace email etiquette tips in this section, the first involves awareness of one's distribution.

Cc, Bcc, and Reply to All – The Bcc (Blind Carbon Copy) tool is a very underused email feature. I regularly receive distributions from professional groups, with dozens of email addresses visibly displayed in either the *To* or *Cc* field.

Email addresses should only be visibly displayed when a)

---

[26] I shouldn't have been doing the newsletter anyway. Part of embracing delegation is having the humility to acknowledge that there are members of your team that are simply better at some things than you are.

When a few team members need a gentle nudge, the Bcc field can be especially useful, especially when combined with a subject line that reads something like this: "If you are bcc'd …"

Schools are busy places, and sometimes team members fall behind on basic tasks and responsibilities, such as attendance or completing a form.

A friendly, low-stakes reminder with a Bcc distribution protects professional privacy while distributing a reminder to multiple individuals.

there are only a few recipients and b) there is an expectation of a group discussion.

By using the Bcc field, senders protect the email addresses of their recipients. But they also protect recipients from receiving multiple *reply to all* responses.

Unfortunately, many individuals either choose to reply to all or have this as a default in their email settings. Coaching team members as to when to use Bcc and to avoid replying to all will help reduce inbox clutter throughout the organization.

One-Source Weekly Newsletters – Earlier, I mentioned the improvements my administrative assistant made to our weekly newsletter. This weekly newsletter was a strategy I retained from my first position as an administrator, when I realized that important email information was being overlooked by several members of our team.

As with any organization, there will always be those

individuals who don't read emails thoroughly. However, it is likely that individuals will miss important information when it originates from multiple sources throughout the week. Along with spam, parent emails, and student communications, teachers and others are often forced to hunt for critical messages within the clutter during their limited and valuable non-instructional time.

Our solution was to move a weekly administrative newsletter, typically sent each Wednesday around noon, hoping that team members had settled into their groove by then.

Except for urgent matters, all communications should typically come through the weekly newsletter, the designated one place for all vital information.

One can always use strategies like one-click surveys to gauge readership, but mostly I trust the newsletter to speak for itself. If someone isn't reading the weekly update, it'll be obvious enough when they start complaining that they had no idea there was an assembly planned for Wednesday afternoon.

Here are a few of our general newsletter guidelines:

- Include a short bullet-point of urgent items near the top.
- Include only brief summaries, hyperlinking to other sources for readers who need more information.[27]

---

[27] Newsletter items often link to an in-depth resource with more detailed explanations.

- Avoid repeating information in subsequent newsletters as much as possible, or place repeated information in a lower section
- Avoid lengthy chunks of text as much as possible.

A one-source, once-a-week communication not only reduces inbox clutter but also allows for staff-wide distributions to be edited for grammar, tone, and length.

Effective Formatting – Writers need an awareness of audience. Electronic messages need to fight for attention throughout a teacher's day of explaining, assessing, managing, and making as many as 1,500 decisions a day.[xiv] In addition to sending messages at the right time and in the right length, formatting is key.

Especially in this age of social media, our brains seem to have been rewired to value the visual aspects of a message as more than the message, itself.

Just as professional speakers will modulate the rate, volume, pitch, and pauses of their messages, the way our words look—the font, the spacing, the formatting—can have a huge impact on how the message is received by others.

However, even from our days as hunters and gatherers, humans seem to be programmed to give special attention to things that stand out from the surroundings.

Noticing distinctions in the environment was a matter of survival—spotting a food source or avoiding a threat—and that vestigial instinct draws our eyes to text and formatting that stands out in chunks of text.

But remember that nuance is key. You don't need to turn

your emails into clickbait. But a little visual design goes a long way.

Written communications can use intentional formatting to help busy readers stay in tune with the message and key details:

- Break larger paragraphs into bite-size chunks
- Use bullet points to highlight essential details
- Use **bold** or *italics* sparingly to emphasize keywords
- Use block indentions to emphasize quotes or illustrative text.

Even though this book is a different medium than a workplace email, notice how these elements have been incorporated throughout the chapters to draw the reader's eye to key bits of information.

Don't Bury the Lede – Sometimes written "lead", the maxim to avoid burying the lede comes from the newspaper industry. The essential facts—the who, why, what, where, and how—should appear as early in the story as possible so that busy readers could get the meat of the story and read further if their busy schedules allowed.

Like a good news story, emails should lead with the most essential information—who, what, when, where, and how. Many readers won't make it past the first couple of sentences.

As an example, of the following emails, the second more directly communicates the sender's needs.

> **Subject: DESE Report**
>
> Jane, I'm working on the report for DESE that is due next week. I think I've figured out most of the form except a few items that Sam will need to answer. However, I can't locate this year's ACT results. Can you hunt those down and send as soon as possible? Thanks!
>
> Revised:
>
> **Subject: ACT Results Needed**
>
> Jane, can you send me this year's ACT results by tomorrow so I can wrap-up the DESE report? Thanks![28]

In the next chapter of this book, we'll look at how professionals can use generative programs, commonly called A.I., to streamline communications and other tasks that keep us from the essential purpose of our roles.

---

[28] Remember to schedule this message to circle back the next morning so you can follow up, if necessary.

- Poorly structured emails and texts disrupt productivity and cause confusion.
- Be mindful of tone, timing, and tool selection (e.g., emails for details, calls for sensitive topics).
- AI tools can help with tone and clarity.
- Respect boundaries by scheduling emails to send during work hours.
- BCC for large distributions protects privacy and reduces multiple replies.
- Consolidate key updates into a single, weekly newsletter.
- Use formatting to highlight key details and improve readability.
- Avoid burying important information; lead with the main point for clarity.
- Communication standards improve productivity, reduce email overload, and support a collaborative culture.

Questions for Discussion

How can setting clear building-wide communication norms improve both efficiency and professional culture?

In what ways might generational or cultural differences in interpreting tone affect communication on your team?

How could you use a one-source, once-a-week newsletter (or something similar) to streamline information flow in your organization?

What email or communication habits do you need to personally adjust to better model clarity, respect, and efficiency?

5

2001: AN OFFICE SPACE ODYSSEY

ARTIFICIAL INTELLIGENCE AS AN EFFICIENCY TOOL

Readers needing evidence that AI systems are tools of efficiency need look no further than the 1968 film, *2001: A Space Odyssey*.

Here's a chilling exchange between the astronaut David Bowman and the ship's sentient computer system:

Dave: "Open the pod bay doors, HAL."

HAL: "I'm sorry Dave, I'm afraid I can't do that."

So, as we venture into this chapter, one thing we know for sure is that AI systems are not fans of open-door policies.

In November of 2022, OpenAI released ChatGPT 3.5 to the public. The response was a brushfire compared to reactions to earlier, more simple versions.

I discovered the tool a few days later when I stumbled upon an *Atlantic* article by Daniel Herman that predicted "The

End of High School English."[xv][29]

Most people are aware by now that ChatGPT is one of many programs that uses *deep learning* to generate text, images, and other media based on probability-based predictions of what the user is seeking.[30]

In other words, it's a fancy autocorrect.

Generative AI programs respond to a user's prompt with the most probable combination of words or image parts based on what its deep learning illustrated about how a human mind might have responded to the same prompt.

Sometimes AI results are excellent. But the internet has a lot of sketchy back alleys, so sometimes the results are ... less than excellent. Such as the time when Google's AI suggested putting glue on pizza to keep the cheese from sliding off. Because, yeah, some guy on *Reddit* jokingly suggested that would be a good idea.[xvi]

This chapter will typically refer to this generative technology as large language models (LLMs) or AI, though the latter term is really more general than how it is popularly used today. Our lives have benefited from less sophisticated forms

---

[29] I published a rebuttal to Herman's essay in the spring 2023 issue of *Momentum* magazine, making the argument that English classes are more important now than ever. https://read.nxtbook.com/ncea/momentum/spring_2023/english_class_in_the_age_of_a.html

[30] Image-based generators work slightly differently than text-based. In addition to being trained on millions of online images, these systems use *discriminators* to fine-tune image production. To make it footnote simple, the discriminator is a system of code that checks image generation against ideal. The better the discriminator is trained on prior images (e.g., what a typical dog looks like), the better it will be in guiding new creations based on user prompts.

of AI for decades (think search engines and GPS).

Current AI technology has some serious limitations,[31] and caution should be used when applying it professionally. However, some applications of generative AI are powerful and, like many other electronic tools, can greatly reduce the toll of tasks on a principal's pursuit of mission.

PRINCIPLE #5 – Generative AI programs, used responsibly, can reduce the impact of tasks on more substantial leadership activities.

The sections that follow are intended to guide readers through several considerations in the use of this emerging technology. This chapter is longer than previous ones, as the final few pages will provide several examples of prompts that school leaders can use in pursuit of efficiency.

Task Versus Formation

At some point in the future, AI may be sophisticated enough to handle most administrative and educational tasks, from fielding phone calls to providing quality feedback on student work.

Those who recoil at the continued development of these programs are right to be concerned about the loss of human agency and the atrophy of professional skills. In his book

---

[31] Including, according to my daughter, the ability to be funny. When she and I were first playing around with ChatGPT, I prompted it to craft a joke about a girl named Paige Allen, this was the output: ***Q*** *Why was the girl named Paige Allen so upset?* ***A*** *Because she has a horrible name.*

Paige wasn't amused (see footnote 21).

Understanding Media, Philosopher Marshall McLuhan wrote, "Man becomes, as it were, the sex organs of the machine world."[xvii]

McLuhan's metaphor emphasizes how our dependency on technology drives the improvement and proliferation of advanced tools. But he continues on to warn that technology shapes us, as well. Many share this concern, warning that advanced artificial intelligence will reduce our sense of agency, our imaginations, and our skillsets.

The existential crisis that many feel is warranted.

I would be a hypocrite if I suggested that administrators should avoid using these tools. Used prudently, generative tools can be powerful ways to free administrators from low-level, time-consuming responsibilities.

On one particularly busy day, one of our students caught me and asked if I would write her a letter of recommendation for a scholarship application.

"Sure," I told her. "How soon do you need it?"

With a nervous shrug, she answered, "Um, it's due today. I understand if it's not possible."

"No problem."

I sent the student a link to a list of questions I have prepared for when students request letters of recommendations. With nearly 700 students to keep track of, I want to make sure my letter doesn't omit key details, such as accomplishments or extra-curricular involvement.

Within a few minutes, the student had completed the questionnaire. Pasting her responses into the LLM, I prompted it to write a letter of support for her scholarship application.

Some readers will recoil from the suggestion that AI should be used to write a letter of recommendation. After all, isn't the student looking for her principal or teacher to pour their hearts into that letter?

I don't think so. I think she's looking for a scholarship to help make college affordable, and without AI, I'm not sure I could have completed the letter before her deadline.

But it was important for me to make sure that the letter reflected my sentiments and my voice, so I took a few minutes for a quick revision. As Tim Cook, CEO of Apple, has said, "technology changes what we do, but not who we are. The human touch will always matter." Using a generative program, I was able to reduce my composition time substantially, but not sacrifice the human touch.

Should Educators Use AI if Students Can't?

In my presentations, I often ask participants to consider whether it is hypocritical for educators to use AI while prohibiting its use among students.

At least in my earlier presentations, the room was often divided, though more participants see a distinction as our exposure to generative tools has increased.

In order to unite the divided room, I would ask my audience to think about the following scenario, which I use to talk to students about AI:

Suppose you are in the weight room, training for the upcoming football or volleyball season. Coach asks you to increase the amount on your dumbbell to 200 lbs. and do three sets of 10 reps.

When Coach isn't watching, you figure out how to rig up a system of pulleys that, when engaged, make it feel as though you are only lifting 50 lbs. You quickly do the three sets without breaking a sweat.

When I ask the students if this approach is okay, they typically acknowledge that it is not. So, I present them with another scenario in which the same Coach asks them to help him with a weekend project to build a patio:

For Coach to lay the paver stones, he needs you to bring them closer to the worksite, as they are currently stacked along the side of his house. You discover a skid loader parked near the pallet of blocks. Assuming you know how to operate this machine, would it be ethical to use it to move the blocks?

When I present this scenario to students, they generally agree that using mechanical assistance would be okay.

Using shortcuts in the weight room undercuts their formation. The athletes in the room desire to be the fastest, strongest, and most agile on the field or court.

Helping Coach with a patio, however, isn't about personal formation but about doing a job quickly and efficiently. It is task completion.

Students and educators should learn to use technology for tasks that distract from deeper, mission-driven work. Artificial intelligence also should never be used when someone is expecting an intentional and genuine effort.

A husband shouldn't use ChatGPT to write a love note for a wedding anniversary. A principal shouldn't use it to write a professional reflection as part of a performance evaluation. A comedian shouldn't use it for writing jokes.[32]

The Strengths and Shortcomings of AI

My initial reaction to the November 2022 release of ChatGPT was a small existential crisis. At the time, I did not fully understand the programing behind large language models. I didn't make the mistake of assuming the program was sentient, as some feared.

> **AI is a powerful tool, but one that must be used with caution due to a high error rate and the loss of our creative instincts.**

However, I assumed these tools would quickly surpass human creativity and logic. As a writer, a former English teacher, and an instructional leader, I recoiled at the idea that algorithms could write poetry as awful as mine.

However, as of the completion of this book, development of AI technology appears to have stagnated. There is a continued expansion of how generative technology can be applied, but problems

---

[32] Okay, so Paige was correct in footnote 31. ChatGPT doesn't have a good sense of humor. After the joke at her expense, she had it write one about a guy named Spencer: ***Q*** *Why did the guy named Spencer Always carry around a suitcase?* ***A*** *Because he had Spencer Syndrome.*
At first, I assumed the program had made up *Spencer Syndrome*. But then I searched it. According to the folks at *Urban Dictionary*, Spencer Syndrome is "when someone acts like a complete douchebag, but no one cares because they always are/always have been like that."

persist with hallucinations and poor logical reasoning.

Some new technological breakthrough will most likely be necessary before the next big jump forward in AI capability.[33]

Until then, we are currently experiencing a horizonal expansion in that entrepreneurs continue to develop clever applications for the technology at its current level.

While several powerful companies are pouring incredible resources into their research, such an advancement could be years or decades down the road.

Despite the initial hype, current AI models are highly limited in the scope of tasks they can perform accurately. Many futurists predict an eventual emergence of artificial *general* intelligence and eventually artificial *super* intelligence, which will move beyond human comprehension.

Until that time, LLMs lack the type of logical reasoning that allows us to have full trust in the output of these systems. This is especially true when programs like ChatGPT are treated like sophisticated research assistants. One high-profile example of this occurred in June of 2023 when a judge sanctioned a law firm for submitting a legal brief that contained several fabricated case citations.

Many businesses that jumped the gun and began replacing human personnel with AI systems, only to find that the

---

33 While the systems are good at generating content from deep learning, LLMs lack the ability to engage in logical processing, resulting in errors and sometimes absurd creations. A substantial breakthrough in neuro-symbolic reasoning (using logic to interact with representations of ideas) still alludes programmers.

automation fell far short of expectations.[xviii]

LLMs are often designed to provide a response for the user *even if* the program has no access to information that complements the prompt.

These error-filled responses, generally referred to as *hallucinations*, will appear authentic and will even include hyperlinks upon request, though the links will generally result in a page-not-found notice.

I often advise users to use generative AI the way one might use *Wikipedia*. While often criticized as a reference tool, *Wikipedia* is an excellent way to get an overview of information as long as the reader refers back to and cites the original sources in the references section. LLMs are also excellent at synthesizing and summarizing long, dense passages.

The more I've used tools like ChatGPT, Claude, and Perplexity, the more comfortable I am knowing the advantages and limitations in using generative programs professionally.

Revisiting the Eisenhower Matrix from chapter two, the highlighted items are just a few of the ways in which where AI has allowed me to substantially reduce my own workload.

While I consider myself at least a B- writer, I have used LLMs in the early drafts of this book. The content is all mine, but I often use the tool to catch errors, for a brainstorming partner, or to provide feedback on completed chapters.

Also, I'm a writer, not an artist, so the illustrations have

---

[34] We utilize an electronic hall pass system that analyzes student patterns and helps us identify the areas of the school that need heavier supervision.

generally come from Dall-E, an image generation tool from OpenAI, the creators of ChatGPT.

	High Urgency	Low Urgency
High Importance	• Observations • Follow-up Conversations • Plan/Teach Class	• Administrative Meetings • Diocesan paperwork • Weekly tactical meetings • Hiring Interviews • Plan in-service • Data analysis
Low Importance	• Supervision • Dismissal • Tackling Email • Hallway visibility[33]	• Mail • Low-level student discipline • Student letters of recommendation • Community Commitments • Thank-you notes

A Few Words about Prompt Writing

Just as coding has become more accessible for the technologically illiterate, prompt writing is less of an essential skill than it was a couple of years ago.

Many new programs have integrated AI in such a way that users can operate without prior training in prompt writing. However, some basic guidelines can help produce better results.

Quick-and-dirty guides to prompt writing generally emphasize key characteristics of a good prompt. When instructing the AI, results can be improved by assigning the program a **role**, a **task**, an **audience**, and a preferred **format.**[35] Prompts can also specify qualities such as **tone** and **length**.

> **Example:** You are a data-analyst preparing a summary of survey responses for a school board. Please create a bullet-point list of feedback themes from the comments I will post below this prompt.

Following this prompt, the user can copy and paste multiple survey responses into the prompt window and then generate a response.

There are other ways to nuance AI prompts, one or two of which I will highlight in the suggestions that follow.

However, even for someone utilizing a program like ChatGPT, sophisticated prompt writing is not necessary for quality output.

Often, it is sufficient to just pretend that the AI is a talented friend you are communicating with. Using a conversational approach allows the program to guide *you* to write an effective prompt.

> **Example Prompt:** I want you analyze survey responses so I can present overall themes to my staff and school board. Can you help me write a prompt for this?

Users who are unsure if they have written a clear and

---

[35] Yes, there is an anagram that would help you remember this—but play around letters, and you'll see the issue. My 5th grade son assures me it isn't a problem.

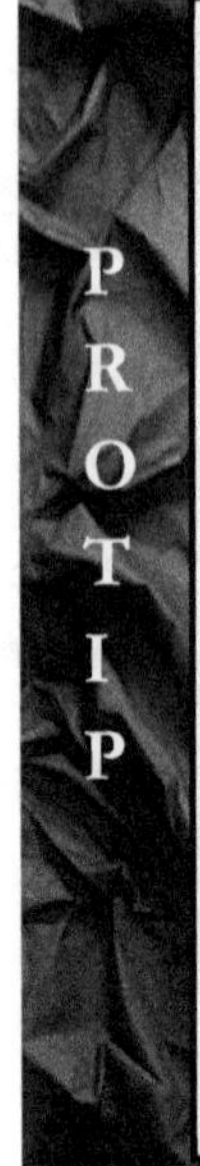

When writing a prompt, it pays to be polite in your prompts: "Please create a …" or "Thank you for helping with this important task."

Some research suggests that AI programs may produce better results when prompts are written politely, possibly because abstract representations of emotional states can affect their responses at more than a statistical level. Polite words and phrases also serve as conversational markers that can help logically structure prompts.

As a bonus, being polite may earn you some mercy when the machine takeover begins.

complete prompt may find it helpful to follow the prompt with a request for the AI program to clarify any ambiguity.

Example Prompt: Before you respond to my prompt, can you ask me any questions you need answered to execute this prompt effectively?

Or:

Example Prompt: Before you respond, repeat back to me what you understand me to be asking so that I can be sure you know what to do?

If the AI program doesn't provide a response that you are happy with, respond as you would if interacting with that hypothetical "friend" on the other side of the conversation.

Continue to ask for revisions until you are happy with the results.

Example Prompt: Thank you for this, but it isn't quite what I'm looking for. Can you revise your response to [insert clarification here]?

Legal Considerations

Protecting Privacy – The recommendation later I describe earlier in this chapter and many of the suggestions below could present privacy issues. Until your school lawyer reviews the user agreement of any professional AI tools you are exploring, you should assume that the 3rd party company that produced the tool will use the personal or sensitive data included in your prompts or uploads.

To avoid this, I will often replace individual's names with generic tags (e.g., "Mr. Namehere), similarly disguising other sensitive information. This allows me to do a find/replace action after pasting an AI generation into my primary document.

Copyright Concerns – Especially with several of the prompts that follow, school administrators and other organizational leaders may be concerned about when it is necessary to acknowledge the use of generative programs. Some may feel that it is not authentic to pass off AI output as one's own. Others may wonder when it is appropriate to cite the use of a program like ChatGPT.

As far as citation goes, the U.S. Copyright office determined that, because LLMs do not have personhood; they also cannot own produced material.[xix] User agreements for most AI programs grant the user ownership over created material. Local organizational policies and style guides should always be consulted, of course.

The legal battle continues as to whether AI companies are guilty of copyright infringement, but end users have so far been held harmless in this battle.

This doesn't mean that a user is free to use a generative program indiscriminately. For instance, it *would* be a violation of trademark to ask an image generator to create a company logo that looks remarkably similar to that of another company.

Acknowledgements – What about a principal who uses AI to write a letter to school parents? Should that letter acknowledge the use of such a tool? Often, this is unnecessary and inappropriate.

Many principals already have administrative assistants or communication teams that will write correspondence, draft speeches, or prepare reports on that individual's behalf.

In many cases, it would be a mistake for an organizational leader to put this type of disclaimer at the bottom of messages: "Composed with the help of ChatGPT." Such an acknowledgement, while true, will undermine the trust that your stakeholders have in your communication skills.[36]

Using ChatGPT as Your Amanuensis

Leaders who do have a strong writing voice may wish to train the LLM to write with a similar style and tone as their other communications, much as my communications director strives to imitate my written voice.

---

[36] Imagine if the President of the United States ended the State of the Union address this way: "I didn't write this. I have speech writers for that." While true, it would undercut his authority.

Example Prompt: I am going to post several examples of my own writing. After I post each section of text, analyze it and write a summary of my style and voice, such as word choice, sentence structure, tone, and other considerations. I am doing this so that you can learn how to compose something with my style and voice.

Generative AI tools are owned by 3rd party companies who *can* use any sensitive data entered unless a contract specifies otherwise.

Once you have repeated this process with three or so of your own writing samples, you can ask the LLM if it has seen enough samples of your writing to create something in your style and voice. It will not be perfect; however, the output will most likely be a strong first draft that you can further tweak for your own needs.

Here is ChatGPT's best effort to imitate my voice and style by writing an introduction to chapter seven's discussion of effective meetings:

> Meetings are like coffee—they can be invigorating or leave you jittery and wondering why you even bothered. We've all endured that endless meeting where someone says, "*One more thing*," and you mentally start calculating how many emails you'll need to catch up on when it's finally over. Or the brainstorming session that's more storm than brain, resulting in a dozen ideas but no decisions.

Meetings have a way of consuming time like a hungry teenager at a buffet, leaving you with nothing but an empty plate of frustration.

Here's the thing: meetings themselves aren't the enemy. A well-run meeting can be a game-changer, aligning your team, solving problems, and inspiring action. The trouble starts when meetings become unfocused free-for-alls or overstay their welcome. For busy school leaders, a poorly managed meeting doesn't just waste an hour—it steals time you don't have from the tasks that truly matter, like being visible in your school or supporting your team.

While I could tweak this into something usable, it's probably not the direction I would go. Before moving on to the next section of this chapter, which gives prompt suggestions for efficiency, feel free to flip ahead to chapter seven to see how ChatGPT's efforts compared with my own!

Prompts for Efficiency

This book and the examples that follow are primarily intended for principals and other administrators. However, professionals in any field should be able to be able to use modifications of these prompts for efficiency in their own organizations.

As always, AI should support—not replace—your professional judgment and voice.

Structured and professional agendas:

Prompt: Create an agenda for a one-hour staff meeting

focused on [topics, e.g., student engagement strategies and upcoming events]. Include time allocations for each topic, a brief introduction, and a closing discussion. The tone should be professional yet approachable.

Observation feedback summaries:

Prompt: Organize the following classroom observation notes into a professional feedback summary for a post-observation meeting. Focus on strengths, areas for improvement, and actionable next steps. Here are the notes: [Insert notes].

Lesson design:

Prompt: You are an educator designing a composition course for juniors in high school. This course will last one semester (January through May). Your goal is to use the uploaded standards to create a course outline that will provide appropriate rigor in helping students meet a variety of challenges that they will encounter past high school, such as engaging in the civic process, communicating at work, and personal correspondence.

Condensed documents:

Prompt: Summarize the following document into a one-page overview. Focus on key takeaways and actionable items relevant to school administrators: [Insert policy text].

Curriculum design:

Prompt: Create a lesson designed to help students analyze the causes of World War I based on the uploaded essay.

The lesson should include formative assessment and higher-level thinking activities.

Planning for professional development:

Prompt: Create an outline for a one-hour professional development session on [topic, e.g., classroom management techniques]. Include a brief introduction, key learning objectives, main discussion points, and a closing activity or reflection exercise.

Analysis of survey responses:

Prompt: Analyze the following survey responses from teachers regarding professional development. Identify the main themes, recurring concerns, and notable positive feedback. Present the analysis as a bullet-point list for a staff meeting. Here are the responses: [Insert responses].

Clear, engaging emails and newsletters:

Prompt: Draft a newsletter for parents about [specific event or topic, e.g., parent-teacher conferences]. Include an opening message in a friendly tone, key dates and times, and a reminder about [e.g., signing up for slots or school policies]. Make it clear and concise, with bullet points where appropriate.

Letters of recommendation:

Prompt: Write a letter of recommendation for a high school senior, [Student Name]. Highlight their academic achievements in [specific subjects or activities], their role as [e.g., student council president, varsity athlete], and their personal qualities like [e.g., leadership, empathy, resilience]. The letter should be professional and formatted appropriately for a college application.

Social media posts:

Prompt: Create a cheerful and engaging social media post announcing [specific event, e.g., the school science fair]. Include a call-to-action inviting families to attend and highlight [e.g., exciting activities or keynote speakers]. Keep it under 150 words and include hashtags like [#SchoolPride, #ScienceFair2024].

Strategic initiatives:

Prompt: Create a strategic plan outline for [goal, e.g., improving student attendance rates]. Include sections for objectives, key strategies, milestones, and metrics for success. Format it as a professional document that can be expanded upon.

Efficient schedules:

Prompt: Help me create an efficient schedule for classroom walkthroughs. I have [number of classrooms] to visit, each requiring [X minutes], with [Y time] available each day. Ensure time for transitions and prioritize visits to [specific grade levels or subjects]. Output the schedule as a table.

Brainstorming partner:

Prompt: Generate creative ideas to improve school culture. Focus on initiatives that promote teacher collaboration, student engagement, and community involvement. Provide 5-7 actionable suggestions, each with a brief explanation of its potential impact:

Report drafts:

Prompt: Draft a monthly attendance report for [school name]. Include sections for overall attendance rates, trends compared to previous months, and any specific concerns (e.g., high absenteeism in [grade]). Provide placeholders for data input where necessary.

Meeting notes or recordings:

Prompt: Summarize the following meeting notes into a clear, actionable outline. Highlight key decisions, action items, and deadlines. Format it with bullet points for easy reading. Here are the notes: [Insert notes].

Compiled and summarized research:

Prompt: Provide an overview of recent research on [topic, e.g., strategies to improve student retention]. Include a list of 5-7 major findings or recommendations. For each, suggest primary sources or further reading where possible.

While A.I. can be a powerful tool for efficiency, generative technology can be an inferior replacement for the amazing talent that already exists among your teachers and staff.

The next chapter will explore intentional delegation as a way to not just pursue efficiency but also transformative leadership.

SUMMARY

- Use AI for routine tasks (e.g., drafting letters) to free up time for high-impact responsibilities.
- AI excels at summarizing, drafting, and organizing content but can produce errors.
- Craft effective prompts by specifying role, task, audience, tone, and format; revise outputs as needed to refine quality and style.
- Anonymize sensitive data and avoid passing AI-generated content as entirely human-written.

Questions for Discussion

How could using AI for repetitive or time-consuming tasks free up more time for leadership activities that require your personal presence and judgment?

In what ways must leaders be cautious to ensure AI tools augment, rather than replace, authentic human connection and voice?

What professional tasks in your current role could AI assist with right now to streamline your workflow responsibly?

How can you help set ethical boundaries for AI use within your organization, especially around issues like privacy, tone, and authenticity?

6

LEADERSHIP ISN'T A ONE-MAN BAND

TRANSFORMATIVE DELEGATION

Our family plays a lot of board games. Among our favorite style of games are engine building games, such as *Wingspan* and *Terraforming Mars*. These games start slowly, but the pace and complexity increase as players accumulate and upgrade resources, increasing the players' ability to accomplish goals as the game progresses.[37]

This is different than some more traditional games, where on any given turn, a player generally makes one move to accomplish one thing.

In leadership, as in games like Wingspan, the goal isn't to do everything yourself—it's to design a system where every player strengthens the whole engine.

Many businesses started as entrepreneurs tinkering away in a garage. But as the visionaries slowly built the right team

---

[37] Currently, though, *Monopoly* is banned at our house. Someone is apparently too competitive and heartless when we try that game as a family. My wife wouldn't specify who she meant, but she gave me a cold glare the last time I suggested, which I suspect means she wants me to look into the matter. I suspect she's referring to our daughter.

and secured financial and material resources, their ability to pursue their vision increased exponentially.

Schools are often transformed in the same way. Principals who micromanage and hold tightly to control risk stifling a culture of healthy risk-taking and initiative.

Several months ago, I participated in a PD session for principals. At one point, the activity facilitators asked each of us to identify one area of needed professional growth. Many among our group indicated a need to delegate more or with increased intentionality.

Some principals serve in systems where there is simply nobody to whom responsibilities can be shared. This is unfortunate, and as discussed in the first chapter, it often involves educating superintendents and boards of education on the importance of providing principals time for instructional leadership.

In other situations, leaders often have trouble letting go of responsibilities. But this attitude betrays a lack of trust in the vision and initiative among the team.

I've often caught myself here, and upon reflection, I realize that I'm acting a bit like Dwight from *The Office*, particularly in the episode "A.A.R.M.", where Dwight names himself his own assistant—Assistant to the Assistant to the Regional Manager.

Finally, there are those empathetic principals who resist delegation because they don't want to shift additional responsibilities and tasks to their already overworked and underpaid team members.

Sometimes, delegation really is just handing off tasks to those hired for that purpose.[38] For instance, the job description of administrative assistants is often to address tasks that would otherwise bog down someone in an executive position.

But typically, delegation done purely for efficiency means using one's team as little more than task carriers. Intentional delegation is a tool for transformation. Trusting and empowering others builds their confidence and skill, and increases team cohesion. Delegation doesn't diminish authority—it orchestrates success.

Those who increase and develop their resource—namely, their faculty and staff—often find their pursuit of mission amplified by the team of leaders that emerge.

PRINCIPLE #6 – As an investment in one's team, thoughtful delegation increases efficiency while fostering ownership and developing leadership skills among stakeholders.

The sections ahead will focus on the philosophical or practical considerations for leaders who wish to improve in engine-building skills within their school communities.

The Economics of Time

The economist Thomas Sowell defines *economics* as "the study of how to use scarce resources that have alternative uses."[xx] The first step in becoming better at delegating is to

---

[38] In a recent census survey of kids that live in my house, I've learned that 100% of older sisters involved in the study reported regularly delegating tasks like dishes and stool scrubbing to little brothers.

acknowledge the increasing scarcity of one's time. Each minute of your day has an alternative use.

At home, for instance, when I removed Facebook from my phone, I suddenly found more time to be present with my family, to read, or stay in shape. I was choosing poorly among the limited options for my limited resource of minutes and hours.

When my wife and I send my older kids on errands or have them take on chores around the house, not only do we free up our own time, but we're helping them make the best use of theirs. What is an errand for me is an exercise in adulting for them.[39]

> **The first step in motivate oneself to delegate is to acknowledge the increasing scarcity of one's time.**

A society runs well when scarce resources are distributed wisely and so does your schedule. When the time and talent of the human resources within a school are utilized with intentionality, the system runs more efficiently and effectively overall.

A helpful analogy involves considering the difference between an orchestra and a one-man band juggling multiple instruments. His drum is strapped to their back, brackets hold a harmonica at the ready, and cymbals clash with each step.

---

[39] Either they learn to handle that task themselves, or they learn to hurry up and have kids to do it for them.

While impressive, the performance has its limits, relying solely on one's ability to multitask.

By contrast, a skilled maestro conducting an orchestra empowers each musician to contribute unique talent, creating a harmonious and powerful performance.

Delegation and Servant Leadership

With his 1970 essay, "The Servant as Leader", Robert K. Greenleaf sparked a shift from the authoritarian leadership style he saw as so prevalent in the corporate world. Servant Leadership, Greenleaf wrote, involved prioritizing the needs and development of one's team over personal ambition.[xxi]

Servant leadership emphasizes leadership behaviors such as listening, persuasion, stewardship, and awareness.

However, it seems like sometimes a misunderstanding of servant leadership stands to undermine the actual goal of this philosophy. For instance, I was once in a conversation with a colleague who talked about regularly grabbing a dust-mop after school to help the custodial staff.

While well-intended, this kind of gesture can backfire—distracting the leader from essential duties and unintentionally undermining the professionalism of support staff.

Setting aside rare cases like staffing shortages or a mess after a major event, this well-meaning act created two unintended problems.

First, using the rare commodity of time to help clean the school comes at the expense of responsibilities only the principal should be handling.

> **PRO TIP**
>
> For complex or long-term tasks, delegation is often more successful when accountability is assigned to two individuals.
>
> Double delegation provides a fail-safe for critical tasks in the event that one team member or the other is pulled away and there isn't time to reorient another individual to the role.

Second, unless there is a critical need, the principal's actions could be seen as undermining the professionalism of his custodial and maintenance team. After all, would the principal ask the custodians to help write teacher evaluations?[40]

I've had just such a situation occur when I tried to chip in to help our short-handed custodial staff by emptying the full trash bins between lunch shifts.

While the act was intended to be a gesture of service, the professional in charge of that area thought I had done it out of frustration because he had been late arriving.

Rather than simply helping with someone's workload, delegation as a servant leader involves trusting team members with tasks and supporting and serving them as they rise to the challenge.

---

[40] There are other legitimate reasons why principals may jump in to help with tasks outside his or her job description, such as to create an opportunity to connect with members of the support team. Stepping into other roles also gives the principal unique perspectives of different operations or services within the system and provides a unique opportunity to connect with the customer base (i.e., students and parents), such as by helping to serve lunch or directing the pick-up and drive-by lanes.

This distinction is central to Greenleaf's 'best test' of servant leadership: Do those served grow as persons?

In his book *Servant Leadership: A Journey in the Nature of Legitimate Power and* Greatness, Greenleaf writes, "Everywhere there is much complaining about too few leaders. We have too few because most institutions are structured so that only a few—only one at the time—can emerge."

Let's pause here and talk about the word "leaders." Not every teacher would perform well as a principal, just talented baseball players don't necessarily make good coaches.

I've known of rock star teachers who crashed and burned as administrators (and some awesome principals who were mediocre teachers).

The two jobs require different skillsets and dispositions.

However, there are many opportunities for leadership within school systems, including department chairs, instructional coaches, and project directors.

Often principals are hesitant to put *one more thing* on the plates of their already overworked teachers and staff.

However, this perspective only arises when one views delegation as passing off tasks, rather than empowering team members to discover the leader within.

A principal who does not delegate (or who micromanages those to whom the task was delegated) is sending the message that other members of the team cannot be trusted to tackle important or complicated tasks.

Delegation and School Culture

Studies looking at professional and personal motivation are fairly conclusive that incentives (either positive or negative) do not generally increase productivity. Rather, incentives correlate *inversely* with productivity in schools and other organizations.[xxii]

If this is the case, then what does drive professional growth and workplace morale?

A close cousin to servant leadership, James MacGregor Burns's theory of *transformational leadership* emphasizes the qualities of leadership that drive the professional growth.

Burns identifies four specific qualities associated with transformational leadership:

Idealized influence – When a leader models resilience during tough times.

Inspirational motivation – When a vision becomes a shared rallying cry.

Intellectual stimulation – When challenges are framed as opportunities to think differently.

Individual consideration – When coaching honors each person's needs and pace.[xxiii]

Burns's work asserts that transformational leaders delegate in a way that is intellectually stimulating and complementary to the individual's unique skillset. Research supports the assertion that, when leaders encourage autonomy and ownership through transformative leadership, employees respond with greater work engagement and trust in management.[xxiv]

Empowering team members builds confidence and skill among others and increases team cohesion.

As Burns writes in his book *Leadership*, "Such leadership occurs when one or more persons engage with others in such a way that leaders and followers raise one another to higher levels of motivation and morality."

Transformational and servant leadership styles are based upon a shift from incentives and other behavioralist strategies. A focus on developing one's team leans more heavily on the principles of self-efficacy.

Psychologist Albert Bandura identified four key drivers behind self-efficacy, which is confidence in one's own ability to accomplish a task or act.[xxv]

Motivation and perseverance emerge as a result of *personal victories* and *vicarious experiences*, such as seeing colleagues succeed at a goal.

Verbal persuasion, such as encouragement and affirmation from a principal or other team leader is a third element that Bandura identified, and *positive physiological states*—the bodily reaction when experiencing success or discovering a breakthrough to a problem.

These qualities thrive in cultures built upon trust and informed risk-taking, as well as self-reflection and collaboration.

Teachers and other staff who are motivated and build perseverance are the leaven in the bread that lift the aspirations and ambition of other team members.

As you think about your own team, as well as the projects on your plate as an administrator, consider the following questions, using the space provided to jot in any thoughts:

- **What is one project or professional opportunity can be shared with team members as a way to reduce your professional workload and foster leadership among your staff?**

- **What team member comes to mind as you think about identifying a leader to share in this responsibility? What qualities stand out with this individual?**

- What opportunities do you have to discuss this emerging leader's strengths and vision?

- What other team members would benefit from working alongside this leader toward the goal you have in mind?

- How will you guide reflection and celebrate success at the completion of the project?

While compensation or other incentives might seem appropriate as a way to celebrate successes when a leader or team reaches accomplishment, Bandura's work suggests that the strongest motivator is the *experience* of the success, along with appropriate affirmation and recognition.

> **"Don't tell people how to do things, tell them what to do and let them surprise you with their results."**
> **– George S. Patton**

Beyond delegation to teachers and staff, one of our strategies at my current school involved giving students—especially our seniors—more ownership in the high school experience.

By handing over control of retreats and school activities, we saw an impressive level of leadership rise among our seniors, and their positive spirit quickly spread throughout the student community.

Delegating with Purpose

True leadership isn't about holding the reins tighter—it's about knowing when to hand them off. Delegation is more than a tactic for saving time; it's a strategy for building people.

When done intentionally, delegation cultivates leadership, spreads vision, and creates a culture of trust.

Revisiting the Eisenhower Matrix again, the highlighted areas are those where delegation has reduced my professional workload (freeing me up for instructional leadership), often while improving the execution of these components of our program:

High Importance	• Observations • Follow-up Conversations • Plan/Teach Class	**High Importance**	• Administrative Meetings • Diocesan paperwork • Weekly tactical meetings • Hiring Interviews • Plan in-service • Data analysis
Low Importance	**High Urgency** • Supervision • Dismissal • Tackling Email • Hallway visibility	**Low Importance**	**Low Urgency** • Mail • Low-level student discipline • Letters of Recommendation • Community Commitments • Thank-you notes

Delegating with purpose can only happen when one hires with purpose. Sometimes administrators realize that they have team members who are unable or unwilling to take on new challenges.

When members of the support team are not good stewards of delegated tasks, the responsibility for any breakdown rests upon the leader's shoulders. Someone did not hire well or has not coached well.[41]

This book isn't the right place to thoroughly discuss how

---

[41] Another factor is community pressure. Many schools employ individuals who are not suited to their roles because of connections that employee has to influential members of the community, such as board members or donors.

to respond to staffing challenges. But administrators who are pursuing a path of servant or transformational leadership should engage in professional development centered around hiring and coaching strategies.

Assuming, however, a willing and able team of teachers and support staff, the following considerations will contribute to a successful process of delegation and empowerment:

Start small – Delegate small responsibilities before handing off bigger projects. You can monitor employees' progress to understand how the new workload affects them. This is a great way to identify team strengths and skills.

Define success – Meet as a team to discuss how you plan to evaluate the performance of your employees. Present them with clear metrics, and explain how you measure success. Employees work more efficiently when they have clear expectations and flexibility. Clear deadlines are important, as are milestone markers.

Match tasks to skills – When possible, delegation should challenge team members beyond the normal demands of their roles. Less than that and growth is unlikely. But a challenge that is too great or mismatched with skillsets is likely to result in overload or burn-out.

Balance the delegation – While delegation should match the team member's skillset, principals should resist relying too heavily on the same individuals. Some support staff positions, such as administrative assistant, exist to take tasks off a leader's desk. However, most other positions in the building already come with several specific responsibilities.

Back off! – Allow your team to complete the work without hovering over their desks. This shows you believe in their abilities and expertise. This is expressed best in a quote often attributed to General George Patton: "Don't tell people how to do things; tell them what to do and let them surprise you with their result."

Encourage employee feedback – Let your employees know you welcome feedback throughout the delegation process. Be clear that you mean to pay attention to the feedback you receive. This process opens your company up to innovation and insights that can streamline processes.

Delegation is an engine-building game. The process can start slowly. However, as *transformational* change happens and more team leaders emerge, the overall organization benefits from a well-orchestrated symphony of collaboration.

- Trying to handle everything alone leads to burnout and reduced quality.
- Transformational leaders empower team members to leverage their unique skillset.
- Treat time as limited and valuable; delegate tasks to focus on higher-priority responsibilities.
- Delegation builds trust, ownership, and professional growth.
- Start small, set clear expectations, prioritize tasks, match responsibilities to skillsets, and avoid micromanaging.
- While efficiency should rarely be the primary goal of delegation, it is an awesome by-product.

Questions for Discussion

How does viewing time as a scarce economic resource change the way you think about your daily leadership responsibilities?

In what ways can delegation be an act of empowerment rather than simply a way to lighten your own workload?

How can transformational and servant leadership principles guide you in choosing which tasks and responsibilities to delegate?

What strategies can you use to ensure delegation leads to personal and professional growth for your team members, rather than overload?

7

LONGER THAN YOU THINK!

EFFICIENCT AND EFFECTIVE MEETINGS

Stephen King's short story "The Jaunt" imagines a future where teleportation allows travelers to cross vast distances instantly. But there's a catch—the conscious mind is unable to endure the experience of an infinity of space-time during the journey.

When 12-year-old Ricky defies instructions and skips the required sedation, his mind becomes trapped in an eternity of emptiness. He emerges from the trip with white hair and ancient eyes. Before clawing at his face, he shrieks to his father, *"Longer than you think! Longer than you think!"*

When I sit in poorly run meetings, Ricky's words echo in my mind.[42]

Chapter six explored delegation as an extension of school leadership, guiding faculty and staff to increased agency in school operations and pursuit of mission. Delegation allows principals to share leadership opportunities.

---

[42] So far, I've restrained from clawing out my eyes after a meeting, but there have been one or two close calls, mostly during HR presentations.

On a much broader scale, well-run meetings are an opportunity for school leaders to reinforce the mission and vision of the organization, as well as the best practices that increase efficiency throughout the entire organization.

Absent of intentionality and focus, meetings are not only a waste of professional time, but they leave important matters on the table that will need to be dealt with at other points, decreasing organizational efficiency and effectiveness.

PRINCIPLE #7 – Efficient and mission-driven meetings fine tune the operations of the entire school program.

The sections ahead will look at administrative meetings and staff meetings, exploring ways that school leaders can best restructure these opportunities for efficiency and leverage them for a more effective program.

The Purpose of Meetings in School Systems

Meetings are where individuals at all levels of an organization's structure allow themselves to be vulnerable and where key decisions are made. Meetings are where leaders can reinforce the mission and purpose of their organizations.

But if those meetings are boring ...

If they are unfocused …

If they lack engagement and accountability …

If they don't drive to closure and clarity …

The professional time is mostly wasted.

There are many excellent leadership books available explore meeting structure and purpose as a key to organizational health. Patrick Lencioni has written several popular books on business management.

In his ominously titled *Death by Meeting*,[xxvi] Lencioni guides organizational leaders to, as suggested in his subtitle, solve "the most painful problem in business."

According to Lencioni, meetings are the most important thing that leaders do. He maintains that it is within meetings that team members challenge and hold one another accountable.

It is essential, for the health and overall effectiveness of a school, that teachers and other staff be aligned with the mission and vision of the school, including the organizational norms associated with those guiding principles.

But books like Lencioni's are typically aimed at a corporate structure, and the nature of school systems presents challenges to effective meetings as they might occur in other organizations.

After all, each teacher is the head of one or more mini-departments responsible for the output of critical essays, nature dioramas, and solutions for X.

Teachers navigate a rigid and demanding schedule each day. What other profession includes a system of bells that throws the entire system into a chaos of reorganization every 47 minutes?

From a leadership standpoint, perhaps a more key distinction with school structures is the scarcity of opportunities for principals to connect with operations managers (a.k.a., teachers). In those rare opportunities for organization-wide collaboration, there is rarely a moment to spare.

Meetings within a school setting take many forms, from administrative discussions to entire staff gatherings. The earlier part of this chapter will look at administrative collaboration, while the final section offers thoughts for staff meetings.

The first step in improving school meetings is to ask *why* the meeting is taking place to begin with. If the reason is to fill a quota of in-service hours, the meetings will be void of purpose. If the staff is meeting for an information dump, the disregard of professional time may even damage the school culture.[43]

Meetings will only be efficient and effective when school leaders practice good stewardship of collaboration time by protecting it from typical meeting missteps.

When I started in my current role, there was a practice of gathering several members of the support staff on a regular basis. This included office staff, the school nurse, the directors of technology and facilities, and individuals from other departments.

Often, conversations would focus on very specific topics

---

[43] While staff and faculty at my current school receive most essential information through our weekly newsletter, feedback has indicated that some members of the professional team value a degree of face time for important items. Next year, we are starting a monthly debriefing—lasting twenty or so minutes—to go over key items for the days ahead. These will not be townhall-style discussions, but a chance for individuals to get clarity and point out any challenges.

that had no relevance to most of the professionals in the room, who sat passively as two or three people discussed the item. What did the two IT guys care about the upcoming Homecoming dance? Why was the nurse sitting through a discussion about graduation set-up?

Reflect on the meetings in your organization. Are they reactionary or planned?

Is the subject of the meeting worthy of professional time?

Will the discussion be relevant to everyone invited to the meeting?

Has engagement and discussion been built into the meeting design?

If planned, do they have a specific and dedicated purpose? For instance, think about the next meeting on your calendar. Which of the following purposes best fits the intent of that meeting?

- To touch base on upcoming activities and important tasks
- To check in with directors of different programs or teams for updates
- To discuss big picture goals or initiatives
- To reflect on the school's pursuit of mission and vision?

Administrative meetings can be for any of these purposes, but combining these micro- to macro-level goals into one conversation is just as much a threat to efficiency as multi-tasking one's way through a to-do list.

The Role of Pushback in Meetings

While the bulk of this chapter discusses staff in-services, regular administrative meetings are essential to strong school cultures.

Lencioni emphasizes that *more* meetings, not fewer, are key to efficiency and effectiveness.

When leaders let mission drive meetings, less time is spent dealing with the headaches, clarification, and reactive leadership.

One suggestion from *Death by Meeting* is especially key to our theme of efficiency: Respectful pushback and healthy conflict should be welcomed in every professional meeting.

This school year, I volunteered to teach a creative writing class as a reminder to myself of what school feels like on the front lines.

Early in the class, I discuss conflict with the students. It doesn't matter how great of a main character you've developed or what the setting is—if the story doesn't have a strong conflict—you'll lose the reader.

Likewise, if meetings are just agreement exercises, engagement is likely to decrease.

Lencioni explains that conflicts make meetings more

interesting.[44] But *interesting* must be balanced by professionalism, because the type of conflict that ensures efficiency is when an administrative team (including any support staff included in the meeting) can respectfully push back on one another's ideas.

Earlier this year, our team explored a substantial change to our summer school program. Some problems had emerged with the traditional model for summer school, but we wanted to avoid trading one problem for another with a rushed fix.

Even small school systems have enough moving parts that the law of unintended consequences carries exhausting and harmful penalties.

Through a series of meetings, we developed a plan that—when rolled out—met with almost no resistance. There will certainly be bugs to iron out, but our team was able to think through the change thoroughly because of one key factor – we were comfortable challenging one another.

In his book *Outliers*, Malcolm Gladwell discusses a cultural challenge that was compromising the safety of flights associated with Korean Air.[xxvii] Co-pilots were hesitant to challenge the in-flight decisions of more experienced pilots. A psychological roadblock prevented them from questioning someone in a position of authority.

Gladwell explains that by putting the senior pilot in the auxiliary position, the instances of plane crashes were

---

[44] I've been at some meetings where unhealthy conflict emerged, and all I needed to enjoy it fully was a tub of buttered popcorn and a box of Junior Mints.

measurably reduced, as the more experienced co-pilot had less apprehension when speaking up.

If participants in administrative meetings struggle to challenge the principal or if the building leader does not feel comfortable diplomatically challenging team members, school programs can not only fail—they can cause damage to the mission of educating youth.

When members of a team are uncomfortable introducing conflict into meetings, it can help to appoint someone to the role of devil's advocate.

Having that be someone's explicit purpose within a meeting allows the individual to model healthy push-back while reducing the apprehension that can come from challenging one's boss or colleague.

Constructive conflict doesn't weaken teams—it strengthens them. When ideas are tested in the safe space of respectful challenge, the school as a whole becomes more resilient and better aligned to its mission.

Five Ways to Derail a Staff Meeting

As someone with adult ADHD, I can say that if the meeting is designed well enough that even I can stay focused and engaged, it's a *great* meeting.

Ironically, as much as teachers are held accountable for lessons that keep young people engaged, the same standard isn't typically expected of the meetings that the teachers, themselves, must sit through.

Principals are called to be good stewards of their leadership opportunities. Remember the definition of economics from chapter six? Every minute that teachers and other staff spend in a meeting is an administrative decision about two scarce resources: the professional's time and the financial resources invested in the operations of that school.

When planning efficient and effective staff gatherings, some principals (myself included, at times) need to keep in mind that meetings bring out the high school kids in all of us.[45]

The individuals in the back of the room are on their devices. The teacher over there is already doodling. Thirty minutes in, Mr. Winslow is already sleeping—albeit with perfect posture.

If this describes meetings in your organization, it's time for a change. This starts by avoiding these five obstacles to strong staff collaboration:

Absence of Purpose – Can every activity or discussion point be tied back to one of three core purposes:

- Advancement of Mission
- Professional Development
- Essential training or explanation

Principals should keep these three guidelines in mind when planning meeting agendas. While a connection to the three core principles can be subjective, keeping them in mind brings intentionality to preparation.

---

[45] High school kids with back problems and mortgage payments, yes, but high school students all the same.

Poor Alignment with the Audience – The default for staff meetings at many schools is to have all hands on deck, while the content of those meetings may only be relevant to a small subgroup.

Meetings might be used to reinforce policies broadly when only a small group of professionals need the reminder. Other meetings might include presentations that only apply to certain grade levels or subject areas. Some training and professional development might not be targeted to the new teachers that need it most.

Overloaded Agendas – Think about that teacher who overdoes class lecture in order to "cover it all" by the end of the semester. Sometimes meeting agendas are similarly packed with all the things.

The director of facilities, the chief financial officer, the HR rep, the counselors, and the librarian all have a "few quick things" to go over with the staff. The principal has planned professional development, and the assistant principal wants to go over several items in the student discipline code. Also, the schedule includes icebreakers and a breakdown of recent test scores. And, oh yeah, we need to discuss whether or not to allow earbuds in hallways.

Less is more in staff collaboration opportunities. The more crowded an agenda becomes, the less likely that staff will have opportunities for meaningful engagement and more likely that essential discussions or activities will be perceived as just *one more thing.*

Many items in an information-dump meeting can be handled by email. Administrators may worry that team members will ignore the electronic communication.

If so, these same individuals are probably ignoring the same messages during long staff meetings, but even so, essential information about policies and procedures can be reinforced in an email with electronic acknowledgement or feedback forms.

Unstructured Discussion – When meetings include town hall discussions of policies or allow for open-mic contributions, the operational integrity of the school is compromised.

Efficient and effective schools have an organizational framework for making decisions and soliciting feedback. It often involves advisory groups, a communication chain, surveys, etc.

Especially among large teams, entertaining unstructured discussions often only engages a small portion of the staff, creating idle time for anyone who has no investment in the topic.

Even worse, by abandoning the meeting agenda, a town hall discussion risk compromising the integrity of the meeting when either the subject or the length of the discussion gets out of hand as dominant voices take over.

Discussions that become town hall meetings also risk harming culture when individuals or programs are called out, putting individuals or teams on the spot.

Lack of Engagement – In the book *Talk Like Ted*, author Carmine Gallo emphasizes the 18-minute rule.[xxviii] According to Gallo, the audience begins losing attention when any presentation goes beyond that 18-minute window. The author suggests any speaker or facilitator keep the 18-minute rule in mind when planning a presentation.

Most school collaboration opportunities last for hours. Sometimes they either precede or follow shortened school days, but often staff gather for in-service on designated days when students are not in session.

> **Ice breakers might bring a few minutes of cooperation, but a genuinely deep collaborative spirit grows through a shared sense of mission and purpose.**

Ice-breakers are not a solution for making long staff collaboration sessions more tolerable, especially when the activity is not connected to the meeting's purpose. While some staff enjoy ice-breakers, others see it as a waste of professional time. Team members might be united in the short-term by a zany cup-stacking activity, but a true collaborative spirit grows through a shared sense of mission-driven purpose.

Opportunities to collaborate and solve real problems together is a powerful social glue among professional teams.

It can sometimes be unrealistic to expect presentations or collaboration activities to conclude in under twenty minutes, as suggested by Gallo's Ted Talk. However, a well-designed session includes variety in tone and pacing.

For instance, suppose the assistant principal needs to

review the crisis plan. Reviewing all the procedures in the plan might typically take forty-five minutes, risking disengagement. Breaking the same presentation into ten- or fifteen-minute sections allows small teams the opportunities to stress-test the revisions by discussing realistic scenarios.

A presentation—activity—presentation—activity pattern works, which is why strong teachers use it to break up lecture in the classroom. As with students, faculty, and staff who are kept in a passive state for too long will distract themselves with other thoughts or activities.

At the same time, meetings can be reshaped to be, not only more effective, but more efficient, especially for principals with large professional teams.

An Alternative Model for Staff Meetings

While some of the pitfalls mentioned in the previous section can be resolved through more intentional planning, sometimes alternative structures better serve the mission of the school than traditional staff meetings.

Bringing professional teams together is a powerful strategy for broader ownership and agency. It is a form of delegation that can include all or most of the organization's stakeholders.

Not only are the suggestions below more efficient than traditional staff meetings, but they present more potential for every voice to be heard and for all staff to feel engaged.

Ad-Hoc Meetings – The default for staff meetings in many schools is an all-hands-on-deck approach—even when only a fraction of the staff needs to be in the room.

For small groups, it is helpful if team members are grouped heterogeneously. Cross-pollinating teams and departments also allows team members to interact with colleagues whom they might otherwise not encounter during regular school operations and brings a greater diversity of perspectives to each discussion.

This can be done by arranging seating ahead of time or through a quick collaborative activity that naturally regroups the team.

For instance, in my presentations on artificial intelligence, I sometimes ask participants to move to a designated section of the room that represents their comfort level with generative AI tools. For the follow-up activity, I ask them to get into small groups that include individuals from at least three of the stations.

Reiterating policies to everyone or hosting sessions only relevant to a few grade levels wastes time and chips away at morale. Match the message to the right group.

These meetings might take place after school or tucked into an in-service day. Anyone with a vested interest in the proposed topic was welcome to attend.

At our school, we are exploring ad-hoc meetings as a way to explore dress code changes or policy tweaks. Team members who are interested in the topic can attend, and others can use the time as they see fit.

Small Groups and Break-Out Sessions – When the

school leadership needs input, small groups and break-out sessions are a good alternative to whole-group discussion.

Most groups contain team members who are hesitant to voice their opinion, as well as those who voice their opinion a bit too bluntly. Newer teachers often fall in the former group, as they are hesitant to make too big of a splash in a room full of veteran team members.

Smaller group discussions are a great way for more voices to be heard as the administrators circulate and tap into table-level conversations.

Team Meetings – In schools where teacher teams have common plan periods, quarterly check-in meetings are opportunities for principals to get collective input from groups of teachers connected by a common curricular focus.

While the principal may have one or two items to bring up during a team check-in, it's more appropriately a time for teams to speak candidly about their concerns or ideas.

As mentioned in the introduction to this chapter, teachers have a role that is, in some ways, similar to directors. Each of them oversees a "team" of young people, and team meetings are a great way for leaders to have discussions that reinforce the school's mission and to seek input from those on the front line of the school's operations.

As this chapter showed, meetings aren't just logistical—they're one of the most high-leverage tools leaders have to increase clarity, alignment, and organizational efficiency. When designed with intention, meetings reduce confusion, streamline communication, and prevent costly missteps down the road.

In the next chapter, we'll zoom in even further to explore how leaders can maximize impact at the micro level—through the classroom visit, the hallway check-in, and the one-on-one conversation.

- Efficient and purpose-driven meetings more finely tune the operations of the entire school program.
- Meetings should focus on advancing the mission, professional development, or essential training.
- Meetings should tie directly to clear goals and include the appropriate audience.
- Agendas should be focused and avoid off-topic town hall discussions.
- Alternatives to traditional staff meetings include Ad-Hoc Meetings, Breakout Sessions, and Team Meetings.
- Productive conflict drives creativity and decision-making.

Questions for Discussion

How can redefining the purpose of your meetings help align them more closely with your school's mission and values?

How might intentional small-group discussions or ad-hoc meetings better engage your entire staff compared to traditional all-hands meetings?

What are the most common obstacles you've experienced in school meetings, and how could you address them to protect both time and focus?

How can you ensure that every meeting you lead or attend feels like an investment in leadership, growth, or mission—not just an obligation?

8

FROM COMPLIANCE TO COACHING

EFFECTIVE INSTRUCTIONAL LEADERSHIP

Here we are. The final act. The Crescendo. *The Pièce de Résistance!*

Instructional leadership is where it all comes together—and where your influence as a principal becomes personal.

As we've seen throughout this book, real efficiency isn't about cutting corners. It's about aligning your time with your highest priorities. And in a school, there's no higher priority than what happens in the classroom.

This chapter focuses on the most transformative, efficient leadership move you can make: showing up often, staying curious, and using short, focused coaching conversations to build a culture of strong instruction.

For those readers who are not in education, while this chapter is very school-focused, the leadership principle is based on the concepts of transformational and servant leadership and is applicable to most other professional settings.

As you continue on with this chapter, whether you work in education or not, continue to ask yourself how you are connecting with your employees and the other leaders within your organization.

Each chapter of this book has emphasized that instructional leadership is a principal's most important responsibility. It should dominate the upper left-hand corner of the Eisenhower Matrix.

My intent with this chapter is not to give an exhaustive review of the current research and best-practices associated with teacher observations and evaluations. There are better books for that, and they are referenced in the sections that follow.

This is a book about efficiency, and as I've hopefully made clear by now, efficiency is not about taking short-cuts, but about applying fundamental principles to the decisions we make about how our time and energy is used as school leaders.

PRINCIPLE #8 – 8. Short, frequent observations, collaboration groups, and coaching conversations align daily practice to the school's instructional values.

There is no strategy less efficient for principals than reactive leadership—running defense as problems arise from instructional or school-culture issues. The sections ahead emphasize a more proactive approach to guiding instructional excellence and collaboration.

Instructional Leadership within Small Groups

Chapter six discussed transformational and servant leadership, through which employees are empowered and supported in professional growth.

Beyond classroom visits, principals shape culture best by showing up where collaboration happens. Attending team and PLC meetings signals that instructional alignment and professional learning are priorities. These gatherings are a critical touchpoint where values about teaching and learning are reinforced in conversation.

At my current school, a moderately large high school, many of the teachers specialize in one department, with a few switch hitters on the team who teach in two related areas.

It is usually possible to align the plan periods so that members of the same department are able to meet and collaborate on a regular basis.

At the elementary level, common plan times might look different, with teachers having a common plan time based on grade levels.

Schools that haven't worked to align teacher schedules miss out on some of the most natural opportunities for peer collaboration.

During these meetings, several powerful things can happen, such as alignment of assessments and review of student progress. Often called professional learning communities (PLCs), these meetings are key opportunities for principals to visit and tap into the discussions at the most local and powerful level.[46]

This is a low-cost, high-impact investment of time.

These are also opportunities for educators to discuss professional reading. While it can be time consuming for teachers to search for relevant scholarly articles and podcasts, principals can assist by identifying material and sharing with team members.

Our school subscribes to the *Marshall Memo*, where Kim Marshall curates top insights from recent educational research and best practices. Articles within Marshall's weekly digest can be forwarded to individuals or departments for whom the material is relevant.

Within team meetings, principals can both learn from and contribute to discussion of how the ideas in these resources can contribute to the pursuit of the school's mission and vision.

For schools that struggle to establish common plan periods, remember that it isn't necessarily essential that plan periods be aligned as neatly as by common departments or grade levels.

Best practices in pedagogy apply to all subjects, and it's a healthy thing for teachers from different disciplines to cross-pollinate with one another. Think of the power in having an

---

[46] I try to avoid using the label PLCs. While a good concept, the rushed implementation of this strategy in many school systems has left many educators wary. It's enough to say that teams are gathering to collaborate without attaching a label that might derail the effort.

ELA teacher and a social studies instructor discussing ways that writing can enhance a history lesson.

Likewise, teachers from different grade levels are able to identify trends in student learning and performance, contributing to the school's work to vertically align standards and assessments.

As discussed in the introduction, some schools face the systemic challenges of budget or staffing shortages. In these cases, there might not be sufficient time during the school day for professional collaboration.

In these cases, it is essential for principals to find opportunities for professional learning communities and other small groups to meet. Some schools utilize early dismissals or late starts as a way to connect as a team.

Peer Observations and Analysis

Not counting my student teaching, I've worked in four different buildings so large that some teachers rarely interacted with others.

In schools, and probably other organizations, geography can create silos among departments.

Often, teachers *think* they know how their colleagues are teaching, their perceptions fueled by student comments. But rarely have many teachers even spent time observing colleagues.

When we started doing peer observations a few years ago, it was amazing to hear the positive feedback from teachers who visited another classroom.

The structure we followed involved having teams of three teachers or staff visit a classroom and document the effective strategies they observe. It's essential that these observations be voluntary on the part of the observed teacher and that the visiting team focus on the positive. It isn't a healthy move for teachers to provide negative criticism to one another.

Instructional leadership involves meeting with groups of teachers and other staff to discuss best practices and student learning.

Typically, our practice is to have the teams observe for around twenty minutes. By that point, they have a strong sense of the lesson and the teacher's strategies.[47]

Following the observation, the team meets discuss the observation with the principal. A team recorder writes up a summary of the positive feedback to provide to the teacher.

When teachers observe each other's classrooms, they get more than just ideas—they engage in a shared understanding of what good instruction looks like. And when principals facilitate or participate in these experiences, it further grounds school-wide conversations in real practice, not theory

Circling back to efficiency, think of the several powerful things that are happening during this activity, all of which

---

[47] While we offer to find substitutes for teachers to do team observations, most prefer to use their plan periods. Planning for a sub and dealing with a drop in instructional continuity is a point of professional stress that many prefer not to deal with.

might otherwise have taken place during several different professional development sessions or meetings.

Consider the benefits from an investment of just twenty minutes with an observation team:

- The principal has direct and intentional professional collaboration time with a unique cross-section of the school community.
- Self-efficacy is developed through the *vicarious experience* of peer modeling.
- Self-efficacy is also fostered for the observed teacher, who experiences a physiological boost of the personal success that comes from having peers provide affirmation of the strong instructional practices that took place during the lesson.
- School culture is strengthened as teachers have genuine professional encounters with one another.
- Teachers have a direct professional development experience that further familiarizes them with the organization's instructional standards.

This last bullet-point is key to the rest of this chapter, which explores the teacher observation and feedback process.

As with the principles in previous chapters, *efficiency* in teacher observation and evaluation is the key to *effectiveness.*

The Evolution of Teacher Observations

A few years ago, I attended a school leadership conference. One presenter, a straight-shooter if there ever was one, used his time at the microphone to challenge the value of teacher observations.

"I don't need to be hounding my teachers with observations," he said. "I hire professionals, and I trust them to be professionals."

While it surely wasn't his intention, he had tapped into a professional struggle of mine. Why do we perform teacher observations? Are other professionals subjected to having a supervisor sit and observe them at his work for several minutes to almost an hour, sometimes having little whisper conversations with the clients? Jotting notes. Scrutinizing.[48]

Why isn't it enough to simply hire professionals and trust them to be professionals?

Good question. Let's pause here for a quick trip through the evolution of teacher evaluations.[xxix]

In Colonial times, teacher evaluation programs consisted of little more the compliance visits from local clergy and community leaders. Were the students getting their chapters and verses down pat? Was Headmaster Crabapple putting the ferule to good use?

From the Colonial model, teacher evaluations evolved substantially over the following decades, bouncing between

---

[48] I realize this chapter is a bit more focused than last ones, with a bit less humor. To make up for it, here's another side-splitter from Gordon Sputtle's efficiency book: "I once tried to streamline my morning routine by brushing my teeth while tying my tie. Let's just say the meeting started with minty-fresh shirt cuffs and a lot of questions."

compliance and professional growth like a pendulum that never quite settles.

What began as moral spot-checks by clergy slowly morphed into industrial-era supervision—where teachers were managed like factory workers and measured by whether they followed the right script.

Mid-century reforms added checklists, rubrics, and bureaucratic layers, giving the illusion of precision while often missing the heart of good teaching. The goal was consistency. But in chasing uniformity, schools often lost sight of professional growth.

By the mid-20th century, educators started to realize what good leaders already knew—checklists don't build better teachers, people do. Models of clinical supervision and human relations theory nudged evaluations toward coaching, but reform pendulums kept swinging. One decade emphasized compliance, the next talked about trust. One prized structure, another celebrated autonomy.

What we've slowly rediscovered is this: instructional leadership isn't about catching mistakes or enforcing templates. It's about being present in the work, asking better questions, and helping professionals think more deeply about how they teach and why it matters.

The result? A hybrid legacy: part accountability tool, part coaching opportunity, and far too often, a missed chance to genuinely shape instructional culture.

So back to my friend on the stage—*why* are teacher observations necessary?

It isn't wrong to say that observations are necessary for quality control. Many professions are inherently held accountable by the public visibility of their efforts. Poorly run restaurants feel the wrath of online reviews. Coaches win games or get replaced. Incompetent lawyers lose cases.

But teaching is something different. The product is an educated mind, and the immediate client is a child.

When ineffective teachers guide a room full of young people, the damage may not be visible for years. It may not be traceable to a specific teacher or practice, as students often encounter multiple teachers, sometimes within the same academic year.

So quality control is a decent reason for teacher observations, but it isn't *the* reason. Many teachers in our schools are models of excellence. Others are good at what they do, with potential to grow stronger. Some, especially those who are new to the profession, are emerging.

The one thing that all of these professionals have in common is a need—and often a desire—for professional coaching.

A Shift from Compliance to Coaching

While the section ahead focuses on a coaching-based approach, administrators do sometimes have the role of working with teachers who are not good fits for the classroom.

A bad chef will mess up your risotto, and an incompetent accountant might botch your tax returns. But a weak teacher can damage a child for life.

In situations when an instructor does not seem capable of—or willing to grow—professionally it is necessary for the principal to shift from a coaching approach to one that will more directly improve the instructional quality for that subject or grade.

In cases like this, following the guidelines of the district or system the principal works in, the principal will need to shift. Observations will involve longer visits, tougher conversations, and more detailed documentation.

This isn't the book to explore that process because there are no shortcuts here. Among the things at stake, such a process should attempt to preserve the integrity of the professional while improving the learning environment for the students.

However, the process described throughout the rest of this chapter allows principals to pivot when that is necessary. Several short, frequent observations will typically provide more high-quality documentation than traditional methods.

During my time as a teacher and my first few years as an administrator, the boiler-plate model for teacher observations consisted of two observations per year.

Each of these observations lasted all or most of a class period. One of the principal's visits was supposed to be unannounced, and the other was an announced visit (i.e., the dog-and-pony show).

Typically, following these observations, the principal and teacher would sit down later for a discussion of what went well in the class and what needs further work. Often, the observation tool involved some type of checklist or rating tool.

When I stepped into an administrative role, I felt uncomfortable with the default model for evaluations, which was similar to the one I'd encountered as a teacher.

Especially when I would observe a teacher who taught a subject area or grade level that I had never taught, I seriously questioned my ability to fairly evaluate the teacher's instructional decisions and lesson design.[49]

The use of ratings and checklists in observations often discourages innovation and risk-taking, emphasizing compliance instead.

After all, I had been a junior high English teacher, so what did I know about band class or teaching students to solve algebraic equations? I'd never once in my teaching career asked my students to sit crisscross-applesauce; yet, I was responsible for evaluating preschool teachers.

My approach to observations began to shift, however, as I realized that I didn't have to be the know-all expert in the room. I certainly needed a good measure of expertise in pedagogy and a basic understanding of the subject I was observing.

---

[49] For the record, I was serious about observations. A friend and I presented nationally on a model we had developed. But nonetheless, I found myself doubting the effectiveness of the practice.

But mainly my approach started to evolve toward one that emphasized a conversational, reflective approach.

In his book *Now We're Talking*, Dr. Justin Baeder suggests a mindset of *curiosity*.[xxx] His was one of the many resources I devoured as I sought a better way to approach teacher observations.

Baeder emphasizes a shift from traditional models of teacher observation and evaluation to one focused on frequent, short classroom visits and driving professional reflection in post-observation conversations.

Another excellent resource is Kim Marshall's *Rethinking Teacher Supervision and Evaluation*.[xxxi] Marshall's book, currently in its third edition, also guides administrators in the practice of coaching teachers through using mini-observations and other evidence of student learning for a more robust system of evaluation.

Marshall also explores how mini-observations can support end-of-the-year summative observations required in many districts.

Books like these, along with my own dissertation research, clearly indicate several qualities of a strong observation and feedback program. The last item in this list of characteristics will circle us back to this book's theme of efficiency.

This Ain't Your Grandpa's Observation Style!

The observation and coaching process should be seen as a principal's pursuit of the organization's mission. As with delegation and meeting design, the goal is not compliance, but transformation.

As you continue through this chapter, think back to chapter two's guidance on block scheduling.

By observing teachers in cycles, administrators can strategically add variety into the placement of observation blocks.

For the first cycle of the teachers on my list, I might choose early afternoon. For the next cycle, I alternate to another time of day, such as right after first bell.

Though often listed at the bottom of a school's organizational chart, teachers are often the most indispensable leaders within a school. After all, nobody ever calls in a substitute for a principal. The school just ticks along. Many may not even realize the principal is gone!

The subtitle of Marshall's book on Supervision and Evaluation hits the nail on the head: *How to shift the conversation to coaching, continuous improvement, and student learning*. A *shift* is key, and over the last few decades, a revolution has emerged in how principals conduct observations and feedback.

For my dissertation, my own research looked into the evolution of teacher evaluations and the qualities that make for a strong program of observations and feedback.

Here is some of what researchers have discovered:

Compliance doesn't work – The 1983 release of *A Nation at Risk*[xxxii] kicked off a decades-long wrestling match as politicians used school and teacher accountability for campaign leverage.[xxxiii] Tough talk among reformers promised that standardized test scores and high-stakes observation models would drive improvements in teacher quality.

But value-added models and ranking systems don't work. Nor does the promise of higher pay or the threat of dismissal.

Teachers go into fight or flight mode and seek to comply. A professional who is looking to comply seeks to fit the mold of a principal's evaluation tool.

This inhibits professional learning and risk-taking. Incentive-based models of teacher evaluation are not only ineffective, research shows they can *inversely* correlate with performance quality![xxxiv]

All of that said, sometimes principals do find themselves working with teachers who demonstrate substantial problems with instruction, classroom culture, or other areas.

Especially when I was at an administrator at the elementary level, I believed strongly that every ineffective teacher who remains in a school team is a year in the life of a child.

Obviously, in the unfortunate circumstance when a teacher either cannot or will not grow, a strong and well-documented approach is necessary.

However, for the purpose of this book, we are going to explore an observation and feedback approach for those professionals in your building—hopefully the vast majority—who are dedicated to personal growth and student success.

Coaching-Based Observations Improve Culture – Craig Randall, whose *Trust-Based Observations* follows the short, frequent observation model, observes that a coaching-based model that focuses on teacher strengths "created an atmosphere where teachers trusted me."[xxxv]

As opposed to compliance models, the coaching approach invites teachers to be in control of the conversation and sets a healthy context in which they can explain their instructional decisions without playing defense.

Further, frequent follow-up conversations give each teacher several dedicated opportunities to talk one-on-one with the administrator.

It's a strong alternative to the more passive open-door policy discussed in the first chapter. Following a coaching conversation, an administrator can do a general check on the teacher's well-being or solicit suggestions about broader school issues or programs.

Coaching-based feedback models drive professional growth – By getting professionals to talk about their classroom decisions and structure in a low-stakes manner, the administrator opens the door for a more productive stepping stone into discussions of professional growth.[xxxvi]

Reflecting upon one's own lesson and articulating those thoughts to another individual, teachers are empowered to evaluate their own lessons more objectively.

Typically, the observation notes for a coaching approach include a simple, objective summary of the lesson, followed by a discussion prompt.

Using a coaching model, principals move into a facilitator role, guiding a conversation that allows teachers to engage in reflexive consideration of their own lesson. The conversation gets synapses firing and creative juices flowing, allowing teachers to look at their own lessons objectively.

An example coaching prompt, similar to those suggested in Baeder's book, would go like this: "I noticed that you changed course during the observation. Tell me about what you were thinking at that point in the lesson."

Even excellent teachers benefit from this coaching approach. Author Mike Rutherford, in his book *The Artisan Teacher*, points out that we improve more powerfully by building upon our strengths than trying to remedy all of our shortcomings.[xxxvii]

"Over the last few observations," the principal might suggest, "I've noticed that you are really good at formative assessment. If you were coaching a new teacher who had a lesson like this, how would you suggest that teacher get a solid read of whether the students were grasping the material?"

Multiple Observations are Essential – This doesn't sound very efficient, does it? Hold on—we're getting there!

Older observation models typically emphasized two visits a year, one scheduled and one unscheduled. The scheduled observation, which often involved pre- and post-observation conversations, is commonly known as the "dog and pony show" among veteran teachers.

Baeder suggests that principals shoot for a goal of 500 unannounced observations throughout a school year, while Marshall suggests a minimum of one observation a month per teacher.

Just like students, teachers benefit from immediate follow-up. Circling back on an observation from several days ago isn't a strategy for strong coaching.

However, I typically do not follow up on the same day as an observation. Teachers may be depending on their plan period or after school time.

I've established a general pattern of following up the next day so that teachers know to anticipate a visit. Often, though, there are opportunities for brief discussion s between classes.

I personally have found a sweet spot in between these two suggestions. In both of the schools where I have served as an administrator, my predecessors struggled to get into classrooms, even for the traditional two visits. Some faculty had to adjust to an increased administrator presence even though we had discussed it at the opening in-service.

Note that the classroom visits discussed in this chapter are not casual pop-ins, but formal observations with a follow-up conversation to follow.

It's a good idea to develop a habit of doing daily building walkthroughs and stepping briefly into classrooms, but this is a practice that should be done in addition to actual observations.

Multiple observations give a bigger picture of a teacher's style. Whether a teacher is observed nine times or two dozen, multiple observations show what that teacher is like on

Monday morning and Friday afternoon.[50] During a science lesson, as well as math and reading. August and April. [51]

Shorter is Typically Better – Yes, observations can and should be efficient. Efficient observations are better observations.[xxxviii]

As Marshall points out in *Rethinking Teacher Supervision and Evaluation*, administrators often experience a diminished return on class-length observations, with most evidence of instruction and student learning manifesting within a short period sampling of the class.

Observing an entire lesson can be beneficial in specific circumstances. Marshall suggests longer observations when a teacher requests the visit or when a teacher has been given an improvement plan or when the principal has concerns about continuity and transitions within lessons.

But, generally speaking, full-lesson observations are challenged by diminishing returns. Barring the reasons mentioned above, very little new evidence of instructional practices and student learning tends to emerge during the back half of a long lesson versus what one observes during frequent observations throughout the year.

---

[50] Teachers should bring their A-game from the first day of instruction until the last. Professional introspection is valuable at any point in the year.

[51] A useful side-benefit of multiple observations, along with casual class pop-ins, is that a principal is often super aware of what is going on in every classroom throughout the building. The coaching conversation contributes to this, as teachers often discuss the long-term scope of a lesson. I've had it happen many times that a parent will have a concern about an assignment, and I'm able to respond immediately that I witnessed the activity firsthand and did not have any concerns.

Shorter observations also fit more naturally into any principal's schedule. In most school systems, barring systemic constraints, a busy principal can work five- to fifteen-minute observations into the nooks and crannies of the school day.

A few minutes in three classrooms a day saves time invested in reactive leadership later.

Plus, the best observation is an observation that *actually takes place*! Administrators who insist on class-length observations, along with pre- and post-observation discussion aren't leading any sort of transformation if they never have time to execute this formula with fidelity.

This is why, along with short, frequent observations, coaching conversations are likewise bite-size, typically asking teachers an essential question and letting the conversation develop from there.

Many questions can guide post-observation conversations, but one of my favorites hits at the heart of great instruction—student learning.

The question is a two-parter: *What are you hoping the students will learn today? How will you know they are learning it?*

The first part of the question focuses the discussion on standards-based instruction. The second zeroes in on the formative and summative instructional strategies integrated into the lesson.

Both are substantially more effective and collaborative discussion starters than reviewing a compliance checklist or going over an observation scoring section.

Other questions can explore the larger context: *Tell me about how today's activity supports your goals for the unit as a whole?*

Or: *Talk about what happened before and after this activity.*

Because teachers often associate observations with criticism, it is crucial for instructors to understand that prompts to reflect on certain occurrences are meant to drive reflective consideration of their lesson design.

And reflection *is* the key. Ultimately, you are trying to guide teachers to a place where they can objectively consider the strengths and weaknesses of the lesson and how it can be made more powerful in the future.

Sometimes, it helps to just ask for that reflection directly: *If you did this lesson again, how would you tweak it? If you wouldn't, then tell me why you felt it worked well as it unfolded during the observation?*

At least a few times a year, I like to give control of the conversation to the teacher, encouraging a more reflective conversation.

What were you hoping I would notice about this lesson?

What are you proud of as an instructor this year?

If you could go back in time to your first year of teaching, what have you learned about effective instruction that you would share with yourself as a first-year teacher?

In traditional models of observation, the onus is on the administrator to do the thinking and talking while the teachers cross their fingers and hope for a good review. With the coaching-based model, the administrator asks the question, listens, and engages the conversation as a way to encourage deeper self-evaluation.

Principals should stay in the classroom long enough to understand the essence of the lesson, the instructional strategies, and the evidence of student learning.

Thorough written feedback following the process of observation and discussion is essential. A follow-up email reinforces the conversation for the teacher and the administrator and provides support for summative discussions.

Still, our leadership practices should be based around helping professionals leverage their strengths and grow through personalized professional development.

Streamlined processes free us from the burden of micromanagement and create space for the deeper work of empowering others. In the journey to strong self-efficacy among your teachers, it is important to remember that leadership doesn't end at the classroom door.

Instructional leadership involves meeting with groups of teachers and other staff to discuss best practices and student learning.

As we refine our approaches at school, we must also take stock of how we lead ourselves—balancing the demands of leadership with time for rest, family, and renewal.

Ultimately, a principal's greatest tool for building instructional culture isn't a checklist—it's presence and collaboration. Whether in the classroom, in a PLC, or in a reflective conversation, leaders shape learning by showing up with curiosity and purpose. Efficiency means more than getting things done—it means doing the right things with the right people, as often as possible.

- Teacher evaluations should balance trust in professionalism with accountability.
- Modern evaluation models prioritize frequent, short observations paired with reflective conversations.
- Effective observations focus on empowering teachers by highlighting strengths and encouraging reflection.
- Focus on short, unannounced visits with timely feedback.
- Streamlining evaluations allows leaders to focus on instructional impact and time for balance.

Questions for Discussion

What are the benefits of implementing peer observations among staff?

How does a coaching-based observation model shift the emotional climate of teacher evaluations?

What are the advantages of frequent, shorter observations compared to traditional, longer ones?

How can reflective questioning during feedback conversations drive teacher growth more effectively than compliance checklists?

How can trust be intentionally built through your observation and feedback practices?

CONCLUSION

FINDING BALANCE

Everything is gradual.

We've covered a lot in this book—delegation, email, meetings, priorities—but at the heart of it all is this: real efficiency isn't about doing more. It's about creating space for what matters most.

That space doesn't come all at once. It comes by the teaspoon. A few minutes of quiet before the day begins. One solid classroom visit each morning. A twenty-minute inbox cleanup. These aren't massive shifts—but over time, they change everything.

When I've made meaningful changes in my life, they've never come from overhauls. They've come from consistent, intentional tweaks. Five minutes of prayer becomes ten. One mile becomes five. One observation becomes a culture.

I've always chased the next benchmark—more results, more outcomes, more output. What I've come to realize, though, is that what I needed was balance. And often, the chaos we complain about isn't just imposed—it's chosen. We say yes to too much. We cling to control. We confuse urgency with importance.

But real leadership means making space—not just for your responsibilities, but for your people, your presence, and your purpose. That starts with a mindset shift: not everything urgent is important. Not everything important is yours to carry.

So, start small. Say no once. Delegate one thing. Protect ten minutes. And then do it again tomorrow.

You won't just be running your school more effectively—you'll be living more intentionally.

Because what we need most isn't more hustle. It's more breathing room. More presence. More time to enjoy life—unscheduled.

Questions for Discussion

What is one small, intentional change you've made—or plan to make—as a result of reading this book?

In what ways have you confused what you "want" with what you truly "need" as a leader?

Which area of your leadership has gained the most clarity through the lens of efficiency and balance?

How might you protect the breathing room you create—so it doesn't get refilled with more busyness?

What does a balanced, purpose-driven version of your leadership look like in daily practice?

The Eight Themes of Leadership Efficiency

1. Inside the office is often where tasks are completed. Outside the office is where the organization's mission is fulfilled.

2. Move from defining your purpose by a list of tasks to prioritizing your responsibilities according to mission.

3. Email and other tools of efficiency, if not managed well, threaten to overwhelm leaders and undermine the organization's mission.

4. By establishing team-wide norms for communication, organizational leaders work toward a more finely-tuned overall system for all stakeholders.

5. Generative AI programs, used responsibly, can reduce the impact of tasks on more substantial leadership activities.

6. As an investment in one's team, thoughtful delegation increases efficiency while fostering ownership and developing leadership skills among stakeholders.

7. Efficient and mission-driven meetings fine tune the operations of the entire school program.

8. Short, frequent observations, collaboration groups, and coaching conversations align daily practice to the school's instructional values.

About the Author

Spencer Allen is a writer and speaker on education, artificial intelligence, and faith-based topics. His book *The Catholic Defender* is one of the most comprehensive books of Catholic and general Christian apologetics available.

Spencer has a doctorate in educational leadership and is principal at a Catholic high school in mid-Missouri and has served on the board for the Missouri Association of Secondary School Principals.

He lives with his wife, five children, and dog.

For questions or to inquire about inviting Spencer to speak in your area, e-mail him at contactspencerallen@gmail.com.

Also by Spencer Allen

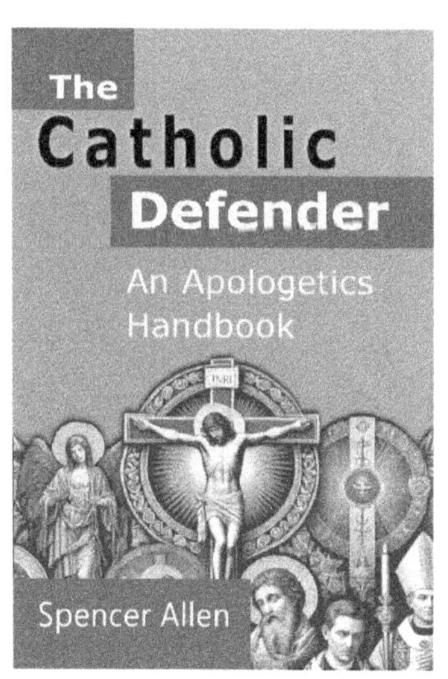

Why doesn't God heal amputees? Where is Purgatory in the Bible? Why is it necessary to confess sins to a priest?

Within *The Catholic Defender*, readers will find a thorough apologetics handbook. Each chapter dedicated to the scriptural and logical arguments behind even the most challenging questions and objections that Catholic might face in conversations about faith.

Each chapter is concluded with a bullet-point summary. Readers will find the systematic explanations invaluable in their own defense and practice of the faith.

REFERENCES

[i] Ferriss, T. (2007). *The 4-hour workweek: Escape 9-5, live anywhere, and join the new rich.* Crown Publishers.

[ii] Deloitte. (n.d.). Workplace burnout survey: Burnout without borders. Retrieved April 13, 2025, from https://www2.deloitte.com/us/en/pages/about-deloitte/articles/burnout-survey.html

[iii] Tracy, B. (2011). *No excuses!: The power of self-discipline.* Grand Central Publishing.

[iv] Goddard, R. D., Bailes, L. P., & Kim, M. (2021). Principal Efficacy Beliefs for Instructional Leadership and their Relation to Teachers' Sense of Collective Efficacy and Student Achievement. *Leadership & Policy in Schools*, *20*(3), 472–493.

Gulmez, D., & Negis Isik, A. (2020). The Correlation between School Principals' Self-Efficacy Beliefs and Leadership Styles. *International Online Journal of Educational Sciences*, *12*(1), 326–337.

Skaalvik, C. (2020). School principal self-efficacy for instructional leadership: relations with engagement, emotional exhaustion and motivation to quit. *Social Psychology of Education*, *23*(2), 479–498

[v] United Auto Workers. (2023, November 14). No union = no rights. UAW. https://uaw.org/organize/no-union-no-rights/

[vi] Detert, J. R., & Burris, E. R. (2023, March 20). When employees speak up, companies win. MIT Sloan Management Review. https://sloanreview.mit.edu/article/when-employees-speak-up-companies-win/

[vii] Bort, J. (2014, May 8). Multitasker test tells you if you are one of the 2%. Business Insider.

https://www.businessinsider.com/multitasker-test-tells-you-if-you-are-one-of-the-2-2014-5

[viii] Baeder, J. (2022). How to schedule & protect time for classroom walkthroughs. The Principal Center. Retrieved from https://www.principalcenter.com/how-to-schedule-protect-time-for-classroom-walkthroughs/

[ix] Clark, M. (2024, December 10). *A workaholic's guide to reclaiming your life.* Harvard Business Review. https://hbr.org/2024/09/a-workaholics-guide-to-reclaiming-your-life

[x] Godin, S. (2024). *This is Strategy*. Authors Equity.

[xi] Madore KP, Wagner AD. Multicosts of Multitasking. Cerebrum. 2019 Apr 1;2019:cer-04-19. PMID: 32206165; PMCID: PMC7075496.

[xii] https://www.emailtooltester.com/en/blog/work-communications-burnout/

[xiii] EmailToolTester. (2025, May 21). Spam statistics: How much spam is there in 2025? https://www.emailtooltester.com/en/blog/spam-statistics/

[xiv] Staff, T. (2022, January 19). *A teacher makes 1500 educational decisions a day*. https://www.teachthought.com/pedagogy/teacher-makes-1500-decisions-a-day/

[xv] https://www.theatlantic.com/technology/archive/2022/12/openai-chatgpt-writing-high-school-english-essay/672412/

[xvi] Kelly, J. (2024, August 27). *Google's AI recommended adding glue to pizza and other misinformation-what caused the viral blunders?* Forbes. https://www.forbes.com/sites/jackkelly/2024/05/31/google-ai-glue-to-pizza-viral-blunders/

[xvii] McLuhan, M. (1964). *Understanding Media*: The extensions of man. McGraw-Hill.

[xviii] Klee, M. (2025, May 17). Company regrets replacing all those pesky human workers with AI, just wants its humans back. Futurism. https://futurism.com/klarna-openai-humans-ai-back

xix https://copyright.gov/ai/ai_policy_guidance.pdf

xx Sowell, T. (2014). *Basic economics: A common sense guide to the economy* (5th ed.). Basic Books.

xxi Greenleaf, R.K. (2002). *Servant leadership: A journey into the nature of legitimate power and greatness* (25th anniversary ed.). New York: Paulist Press, 27.

xxii Amrein-Beardsley, A., Lavery, M. R., Holloway, J., Pivovarova, M., & Hahs-Vaughn, D. L. (2023). Evaluating the validity evidence surrounding the use of value-added models to evaluate teachers: A systematic review. *Education Policy Analysis Archives, 31*(117–118), 1–38. https://doi.org/10.14507/epaa.31.117-118

Brady, M. P. (2021). An alternative, curriculum-based value-added model for teacher preparation programmes: A research summary. *Educational Review, 73*(5), 544–562. https://doi.org/10.1080/00131911.2020.1868950

Darling-Hammond, L., Amrein-Beardsley, A., Haertel, E., & Rothstein, J. (2012). Evaluating teacher evaluation. *Phi Delta Kappan, 93*(6), 8–15. https://doi.org/10.1177/003172171209300603

Kohn, A. (2018). *Punished by rewards: The trouble with gold stars, incentive plans, A's, praise, and other bribes* (25th anniversary ed.). Mariner Books.

Buckingham, M., & Goodall, A. (2023). The feedback fallacy. *Physician Leadership.* https://www.physicianleaders.org/articles/the-feedback-fallacy

xxiii Northouse, P. G. (2022). *Leadership: Theory and Practice* (9th ed.). Thousand Oaks, CA: Sage.

xxiv Hoch, J. E., W. H. Bommer, J. H. Dulebohn, and D. Wu. 2018. "Do Ethical, Authentic, and Servant Leadership Explain Variance Above and Beyond Transformational Leadership? A Meta-Analysis." Journal of Management 44 (2): 501–529. doi:10.1177/0149206316665461.

xxv Bandura, A. (2000), "Cultivate self-efficacy for personal and organizational effectiveness," in Locke, E.A. (Ed.), *The Blackwell*

Handbook of Principles of Organizational Behavior, Oxford, Malden, MA, pp. 120-36.

[xxvi] Lencioni, P. *Death by Meeting: A Leadership Fable about Solving the Most Painful Problem in Business*, Jossey-Bass; 1st edition, 2004.

[xxvii] Gladwell, M. (2008). *Outliers: The story of success.* Little, Brown and Company.

[xxviii] Gallo, C. (2014). *Talk like TED: The 9 public-speaking secrets of the world's top minds.* St. Martin's Press.

[xxix] Goldstein, D. (2015). The teacher wars: A history of America's most embattled profession. Anchor Books.

Jewell, J. W. (2017). From inspection, supervision, and observation to value-added evaluation: A brief history of U.S. teacher performance evaluations. Drake Law Review, 65, 363–401.

Tracy, S. J. (1995). How historical concepts of supervision relate to supervisory practices today. The Clearing House: A Journal of Educational Strategies, Issues, and Ideas, 68(5), 320–325. https://doi.org/10.1080/00098655.1995.9957849

Ravitch, D. (2014). *Reign of error: The hoax of the privatization movement and the danger to America's public schools.* Vintage Books.

[xxx] Baeder, J. (2018). *Now we're talking! 21 days to high-performance instructional leadership.* Solution Tree Press.

[xxxi] The Marshall, K. (2024). *Rethinking teacher supervision and evaluation: How to shift the conversation to coaching, continuous improvement, and student learning* (3rd ed.). Jossey-Bass.

[xxxii] U.S. Department of Education, National Commission on Excellence in Education. (1983). *A Nation at Risk: The Imperative for Educational Reform.* Retrieved December 19, 2023, from https://edreform.com/wp-content/uploads/2013/02/A_Nation_At_Risk_1983.pdf

[xxxiii] Ravitch, D. (2000). *Left back: A century of battles over school reforms.* Simon & Schuster.

[xxxiv] Amrein-Beardsley, A., Lavery, M. R., Holloway, J., Pivovarova, M., & Hahs-Vaughn, D. L. (2023). Evaluating the validity evidence surrounding the use of value-added models to evaluate teachers: A systematic review. *Education Policy Analysis Archives, 31*(117–118), 1–38. https://doi.org/10.14507/epaa.31.117-118

Darling-Hammond, L., Amrein-Beardsley, A., Haertel, E., & Rothstein, J. (2012). Evaluating teacher evaluation. *Phi Delta Kappan, 93*(6), 8–15. https://doi.org/10.1177/003172171209300603

Hill, A. J., & Jones, D. B. (2021). Paying for whose performance? Teacher incentive pay and the Black–White test score gap. *Educational Evaluation and Policy Analysis, 43*(3), 445–471. https://doi.org/10.3102/01623737211012752

Kohn, A. (2018). *Punished by rewards: The trouble with gold stars, incentive plans, A's, praise, and other bribes* (25th anniversary ed.). Mariner Books.

Buckingham, M., & Goodall, A. (2023). The feedback fallacy. *Physician Leadership.* https://www.physicianleaders.org/articles/the-fe Trust Based. (n.d.). Trust-Based Observations: Maximizing teaching & learning growth. https://trustbased.com/edback-fallacy

[xxxv] Trust Based. (n.d.). *Trust-Based Observations: Maximizing teaching & learning growth.* https://trustbased.com/

[xxxvi] Blase, J., & Blase, J. (2000). Effective instructional leadership: Teachers' perspectives on how principals promote teaching and learning in schools. Journal of Educational Administration, 38(2), 130–141. https://doi.org/10.1108/09578230010320082

Palmisano, A. J. (2018). Does evaluation affect teacher self-efficacy? A qualitative investigation into the effects of evaluation on teachers' sense of efficacy [Doctoral dissertation, ProQuest Information & Learning]. Dissertation Abstracts International Section A: Humanities and Social Sciences, 78(11–A(E)).

Randall, C. (2020). There's a better way: Trust-based observations. Education Week. Retrieved from https://www.edweek.org/education/opinion-theres-a-better-way-trust-based-observations/2020/10

Marshall, K. (2024). Mini-Observations 2.0. Phi Delta Kappan, 105(7), 52–57. https://doi.org/10.1177/0031721724121234

Thornton, B., Zunino, B., & Beattie, J. W. (2020). Moving the dial: Improving teacher efficacy to promote instructional change. Education, 140(4), 171–180.

[xxxvii] Rutherford, M. (2013). *The Artisan Teacher*. A field guide to skillful teaching. Rutherford Learning Group.

[xxxviii] Marshall, K., & Marshall, D. (2017). Mini-observations: A keystone habit. School Administrator, 74(11), 26–29.

Neumerski, C. M., Grissom, J. A., Goldring, E., Rubin, M., Cannata, M., Schuermann, P., & Drake, T. A. (2018). Restructuring instructional leadership: How multiple-measure teacher evaluation systems are redefining the role of the school principal. Elementary School Journal, 119(2), 270–297.

www.ingramcontent.com/pod-product-compliance
Lightning Source LLC
LaVergne TN
LVHW020718110826
845149LV00012B/2322

* 9 7 9 8 9 9 2 9 3 2 6 1 4 *